Intimate
Friendship
with GOD

Other Titles by Joy Dawson

The Fire of God

This enlightening, challenging, encouraging book explains how we can come through the inevitable heat of life's circumstances more like Jesus, but unscarred by the flames.

Jesus, the Model: The Plumb Line for Christian Living

Becoming more like Jesus—radically real—we discover our greatest challenge and ultimate fulfillment.

Forever Ruined for the Ordinary

This exciting book explains how to experience the adventure of hearing and obeying God's voice as a way of life.

Intercession, Thrilling and Fulfilling

An inspiring manual taking the reader to greater depths and breadth in effective prayer for others.

Some of the Ways of God in Healing

If you have more questions than answers about healing, then this book is for you. Joy is ruthless in her pursuit of truth from God's Word.

Influencing Children to Become World Changers

Filled with wisdom, inspiration, and fascinating real-life stories, this practical book is a must-read for everyone who desires to impact children to enable them to reach their God-ordained destinies and help shape the world.

Intimate
Friendship
with GOD

Through Understanding the Fear of the Lord

Revised Edition

JOY DAWSON

Chosen
Grand Rapids, Michigan

Published by Chosen Books
A division of Baker Publishing Group
P.O. Box 6287, Grand Rapids, MI 49516-6287
www.chosenbooks.com

Revised edition published 2008

Second printing, September 2008

Printed in the United States of America

Library of Congress Cataloging-in-Publication Data
Dawson, Joy.
   Intimate friendship with God : through understanding the fear of the Lord
/ Joy Dawson. — Rev. ed.
      p.   cm.
   ISBN 978-0-8007-9441-5 (pbk.)
   1. Christian life. 2. Fear of God—Christianity. I. Title.
BV4501.3.D394 2008
248.4—dc22   2007042661

Unless otherwise indicated, all Scripture is taken from the New Revised Standard
Version of the Bible, copyright 1989, Division of Christian Education of the National
Council of the Churches of Christ in the United States of America. Used by permis-
sion. All rights reserved.

Scripture marked AMP is taken from the Amplified® Bible, Copyright © 1954, 1958,
1962, 1964, 1965, 1987 by The Lockman Foundation. Used by permission.

Scripture marked NIV is taken from the HOLY BIBLE, NEW INTERNATIONAL
VERSION®. NIV®. Copyright © 1973, 1978, 1984 by International Bible Society.
Used by permission of Zondervan. All rights reserved.

Scripture marked NKJV is taken from the New King James Version. Copyright © 1982
by Thomas Nelson, Inc. Used by permission. All rights reserved.

Scripture marked KJV is taken from the King James Version of the Bible.

The excerpt on pages 72–73 was written by M. R. De
Haan II, from *Our Daily Bread*, copyright 1983 by *Radio
Bible Class*. Used by permission.

Materials from *The Fire of God* by Joy Dawson, copyright
2005, used by permission of Destiny Image Publishers,
167 Walnut Bottom Road, Shippensburg, PA 17257.
www.destinyimage.com.

In keeping with biblical principles of
creation stewardship, Baker Publishing Group advocates the responsible
use of our natural resources. As a
member of the Green Press Initiative,
our company uses recycled paper
when possible. The text paper of
this book is comprised of 30% post-
consumer waste.

To my outstanding Christian parents, John and Grace Manins, who greatly influenced my early life in relation to the fear of the Lord.

To my beloved husband, Jim, who continues to be my lifelong closest companion.

To my dearest children, John and Jillian, and their wonderful partners, Julie Dawson and John Bills.

To my precious grandchildren and their wonderful partners, David and Kati Dawson, Paul and Amber Dawson, Matthew and Korah Dawson, Rachel Dawson, Jenny and Raphael Gruenenwald and Justin Bills.

These are all my treasured friends.

Contents

Acknowledgments 9
Foreword 11
Preface 15

1. What Is the Fear of the Lord? 17
2. Obedience Because of Who God Is 29
3. Release from the Fear of Man 45
4. The Importance of God's Holiness 61
5. Different Levels in Our Attitude toward Sin 67
6. True Repentance 73
7. How Do We Repent? 83
8. Other Influences That Affect Our Choices 89
9. Our Thought Lives 99
10. Relationships: Holy or Unholy 109
11. God's Gift of Sex 117
12. The Power of a Woman's Influence 125
13. Touching the Lord's Anointed 131
14. Encouragement 143
15. Idolatry and the Fear of the Lord 147
16. What It Takes to Obtain the Fear of the Lord 155
17. The Source of Wisdom 163
18. Rewards for Those Who Fear the Lord 169

What a Commitment of Life to the Lord Jesus Christ
    Means 179
Essentials for Progress as a Christian 183

Acknowledgments

My sincere gratitude goes to my beloved husband for his willingness to listen and comment during this writing project, and then to type up my handwritten scripts. My deepest appreciation is for the way he has covered this revised edition so faithfully in intercession. And exactly the same appreciation goes to my dear intercessor friends.

I am very grateful to Pastor Jack Hayford for his encouraging remarks in the foreword. It has also been a joy to work with Jane Campbell, who had the vision for this updated version.

I also want to honor the following people who helped in various ways with the original edition of this book over twenty years ago: Janet Lambert, Teresa Gelini, Molly Farlow, Bob Owen, Evelyn Wheeler, John Mauldin and Leonard LeSourd.

Foreword

We live in a day when it is increasingly difficult to get people to think seriously about anything—often not even about themselves or their own lives. If urged to think, the person may look as blank as though he or she had just been asked to give the exact time in Beijing.

I do not mean to be either critical or condescending of the present dumbing down of our culture, but we are surrounded by habits of thoughtlessness. This book is an invitation to a different lane of traffic, calling you and me beyond a society drowning in sound bites, jiving to its iPods, clicking its way through an endless selection of websites and popping off inane emails.

Not everyone, of course—not at all. And frankly, without seeming to attempt to schmooze you, I have to say that the above is probably not true of you. Anyone who bothers to open a book that so clearly says, "God is here!" is surely willing to think—or, better, to think seriously. So here is a pair of thoughts by way of introduction.

First, this book is about fearing God, using straight talk about the Creator without insipid terms or mystical ideas. The "fearing God" idea is not as some might think, posing God as arbitrary, monstrous or tyrannical, as though He were a Norwegian deity perched on a mountaintop with a handful of lightning bolts. Instead, the opposite becomes apparent—and this might seem trite—that God is *love* (a statement that needs to be kept galaxies distant from the syrupy notion that "love is God"). A staggering fact will begin to unfold here: You will find that the fear of God actually leads to a kind of real-life love affair. If that sounds incongruous, you will be helped to "think about it."

Second, any book reader does well to think about who the writer is. And I am honored to introduce you to Joy Dawson—practical as a housewife, witty as a speaker, insightful as a prophet and as simply profound as a good theologian. I have known her for more than thirty years, and the most amazing thing to me about her is her effectiveness at helping people to *think straight.* Her writings, teachings, recordings and seminars around the world have influenced millions of all ages, but most impressive to me is her ability to attract the minds of inquiring college-age and young adults—ones who not only want to think, but are tired of *not* thinking.

So, move ahead into these pages with Joy. You will find that she brings great clarity and sensible purpose to . . . well, to understanding the concept of fearing God. And even though this book is about thinking, it is not about finding God via a complex, mazelike mind trip. To the contrary, you will soon discover that it is amazingly simple (though not simplistic). Here is a way toward *thinking straight* about God that will result in living, loving and learning life at its fullest and best.

—Jack W. Hayford
President, International Foursquare Churches
Founding pastor, The Church On The Way
Chancellor, The King's College and Seminary

Preface

Intimate friendship with God. What a mind-boggling concept! The more we understand what God is really like, the prospect of the fulfillment of that concept becomes most exciting.

To have a nodding acquaintance with the Creator of the universe is no small thought. But to be on intimate terms with Him is enough to give us heart flutters for the rest of our lives.

Multiplied millions of people believe that God is the Creator of the universe, but fewer experience the wonderful relationship of Him as Father—which is where the intimacy starts.

The excitement and fulfillment from experiencing close friendship with God has to start with becoming part of God's family. We have to be individually linked to Him through a personal relationship with His Son, the Lord Jesus Christ.

In the section at the back of this book, titled "What a Commitment of Life to the Lord Jesus Christ Means," I have given the reader the simple but definite steps to take from God's Word in order for that relationship to begin. There is also practical instruction on "Essentials for Progress as a Christian." I would urge you to read it through carefully and make application where necessary.

Once we have been born again into the family of God, the Holy Spirit is then able to give us the understanding of how we can progressively find fulfillment in the most exciting relationship of our lives—friendship with God.

—Joy Dawson

1

What Is the Fear of the Lord?

When Adam and Eve took their first bites of the forbidden fruit in the Garden of Eden, they really started something . . .

something you and I do not need to perpetuate;

something you and I with our free wills can choose not to do;

something for which we can actually have a hatred;

something we can resist when under the strongest and subtlest temptations of Satan

. . . because there is something else God has made available to us.

It is the most foolproof thing in the world in relation to sinning; it is called the fear of the Lord.

Before you read further, I suggest we pray this prayer together:

We would be still and know that You are God—King God, supreme in Your authority, the ruling, reigning monarch of this universe, timeless in Your existence, ingenious in Your creativity and with totality of ownership. We stand in awe of You, as we contemplate Your awesome holiness, majestic splendor, blazing glory, limitless power and unquestionable sovereignty. We worship You for Your flawless character, Your infinite knowledge and wisdom, Your absolute justice, unswerving faithfulness, unending mercy, matchless grace and terrible wrath against sin. We bow our hearts and bend our knees before You as we acknowledge Your dazzling beauty, Your fascinating personality, Your incomprehensible humility, Your unsearchable understanding and Your unfathomable love. We acknowledge that our greatest need is to have a far greater revelation of what You are really like. We ask You to meet that need. We would also join with Moses and pray, "Teach us Your ways, that we may know You and find favor in Your sight." Thank You that You will answer these sincere requests, in Jesus' name. Amen.

The fear of the Lord is undoubtedly one of the most important of God's ways; that is why this book is devoted to its discovery.

We need to understand what the fear of the Lord *is* in order to understand what it is *not*.

Proverbs 8:13 says, "The fear of the LORD is hatred of evil"; that means having God's attitude toward sin at all times. The more we study the holiness of God from His Word, the more we will understand the extent of His hatred of sin.

God has no tolerance toward sin; therefore, He will not compromise with it. Sin is abhorrent to His very nature. The

One who created us and longs for us to be fulfilled through intimate friendship with Himself says, "You shall be holy; for I the LORD your God am holy" (Leviticus 19:2). Therefore, understanding what it means to hate sin is of primary importance in order to fulfill that command.

We can be assured that because God is just, He would never set us a standard without making full provision for us to attain it.

No matter how unholy we are now, or how impossible it may seem for us to become holy, if we have committed our lives to the Lord Jesus Christ and He is living within us, we need to remember *He* is holy. If we choose to walk in obedience to revealed truth and the next thing He tells us to do, His holy life will start to be manifest through us.

Another definition of the fear of the Lord is given in Malachi chapter 2, where God is making reference to Levi the priest. In verse five He says, "My covenant with him was a covenant of life and peace, and I gave them to him, that he might fear; and he feared me, he *stood in awe of my name*" (italics added).

What is His name, that we are to stand in awe of as part of the fear of the Lord?

God's most dynamic, two-word description of Himself is, unquestionably, "I AM" (Exodus 3:14), meaning He is *everything* that is perfect and excellent and complete and flawless;

EVERYTHING we will ever need Him to be to fulfill us;

EVERYTHING we will ever need for Him to work in us in order to conform us to the image of His dear Son;

19

EVERYTHING we will ever need to work through us to make Him known to others.

He tells us to stand in awe of a Being who is so completely, comprehensively, supremely and totally sufficient; who always has been, is now and always will be so perfect that there is no way to describe Him other than I AM.

We pause to meditate, realizing with reverential awe in our hearts that He is waiting for us to give Him the only response of true faith—

You are! You are! You are!

The Word of God takes on new meaning as we hear the Holy Spirit echoing into our minds and memories:

> He is my light and my salvation.
> He is my strength.
> He is my Rock and refuge.
> He is my fortress and deliverer.
> He is my shield and buckler.
> He is my great High Priest and intercessor.
> He is my King and my God.
> He is my lover.
> He is mine and I am His!

The following verses give another dimension of the fear of the Lord: "Let all the earth fear the LORD, let all the inhabitants of the world stand in awe of him! For he spoke, and it came to be; he commanded, and it stood forth" (Psalm 33:8–9).

This means that we are to stop and consider, with awe and wonder, the limitless power and supreme authority of one who, by His spoken words alone, has brought the universe into being. And Hebrews 1:3 tells us that by that same word of power the universe is being upheld. More than that, 2 Peter 3:7 says, "But by the same word the heavens and earth that now exist have been stored up for fire, being kept until the day of judgment and destruction of ungodly men." Then, in verse thirteen, we are told to wait for the new heavens and a new earth where righteousness dwells.

So by spoken words our God creates, holds together, destroys and re-creates heavens and earth. That is real power! Almighty power! God power!

David came to understand how these aspects of the fear of the Lord heightened the worship and praise he was able to experience and express. He says, "I will tell of thy name to my brethren; in the midst of the congregation I will praise thee: You who fear the LORD, praise him! all you sons of Jacob, glorify him, and stand in awe of him, all you sons of Israel!" (Psalm 22:22–23).

So the fear of the Lord should produce in us the same attitude toward sin that God has, which is to hate it. It should also give us a deep respect for and understanding of the holiness of God, the power of God and the sufficiency of God to meet man's need.

And there is more. We need to take God a lot more seriously. There is a sense in which it is spiritually healthy to be afraid of God—like when Jesus said in Matthew 10:26–27, "For nothing is covered that will not be revealed, or hidden that will not be known. What I tell you in the dark, utter in the light; and what you hear whispered, proclaim upon the housetops." Listen to what follows that awesome prediction and injunction. "And do not fear those who kill the body but cannot kill the soul; rather fear him who can destroy both soul and body in hell" (verse 28).

When people treat God like or often less than other human beings, there is no understanding whatsoever of the fear of the Lord upon them. To put it very colloquially, the more we really know God, the more we understand that we do not mess with Him. No sir! No way! No time!

In fact the Bible proves that when God really puts His holiness and glory on display, as in genuine revival, death can be the penalty among the church folk for lying and disobedience to the Holy Spirit. It was with Ananias and his wife, Sapphira, in Acts 5:1–10. The results are very significant among both the Christians and non-Christians. Verse eleven says, "And great fear came upon the whole church, and upon all who heard of these things." In other words, they were scared spitless! Then verse thirteen says, "None of the rest dared join them, but the people held them in high honor." Outsiders took the early Church "dead" seriously!

What do you think God means when He tells us to tremble before Him? And why? In Psalm 99:1, we read, "The LORD reigns; let the peoples tremble!" Verse 3 says, "Holy is he!" So we are exhorted to take God's supreme authority and pristine purity so seriously that we tremble in His awesome presence. Do we? Ever? There is a strong exhortation to those in leadership regarding this truth in Psalm 2:10–11: "Now therefore, be wise, O kings; be instructed, you judges of the earth. Serve the LORD with fear, and rejoice with trembling" (NKJV).

David the psalmist understood this concept from his life of studying God's Word when he said, "My flesh trembles for fear of You, and I am afraid of Your judgments" (Psalm 119:120, NKJV). This kind of genuine fear of the Lord is, sadly, greatly missing in the Body of Christ today, to our detriment.

God wonders why we have so little genuine fear of the Lord when He asks the question in Jeremiah 5:22, "Do you not fear me? says the LORD; do you not tremble before me? I placed the sand as the bound for the sea, a perpetual barrier which it cannot pass." The more foreign all this may sound, the more we should understand how far we are removed from living in the fear of the Lord. And the more we should cry out to God to show us how to live by the standard of His Word. He will always reward that cry with revelation of truth.

In Jeremiah 9:23–24, we are told to glory only in the understanding that we have of the knowledge of God, and that His three main attributes are steadfast love, justice and righteousness. When we have understanding of God's unconditional love for us, demonstrated by the price He paid for our redemption at Calvary, we will always feel secure. We know that we can approach Him at any time. When we have revelation of God's judgment and justice, along with His holiness, we will realize how we need to understand the importance of the fear of the Lord, and how it works in daily living. Through His love we have acceptance. Through the fear of the Lord operating in our lives, we have His favor. There is a big difference.

What I am now going to share happened on a Saturday night at a church singles' retreat when the liturgy was at zero dimensions, which made it much easier for the breakthrough we experienced. First, I gave an in-depth teaching from God's Word on the justice of God, after which opportunity was given for the audience to openly respond. Several shared genuine deep needs to which I responded with compassionate counsel. At the same time, I called everyone to participate by being conduits of the caring love of God toward the hurting individuals—the love of God being the most powerful source of healing. The Holy Spirit was stretching the audience in the areas of compassion and patience. He also had rewards in mind.

God then directed me to share the following Scriptures.

Psalm 99:1: "The LORD reigns; let the peoples tremble!"

Ezra 9:4: "Then all who trembled at the words of the God of Israel . . . gathered round me [Ezra]."

Ezra 10:3: "Those who tremble at the commandment of our God; and let it be done according to the law."

Next, the Holy Spirit directed me to call everyone to stand at full attention, as we would if an earthly monarch were to enter the room. We did this with our eyes closed for about fifteen to twenty minutes. We focused our worship specifically on God's majestic splendor, awesome holiness and blazing glory—in total silence! This resulted in a visitation of the Lord's awesome presence, which was manifest in numbers of ways to His waiting people. Several, including the executive pastor of the church, had a vision of the Lord Jesus in a long robe, walking between the rows of people, while His robe brushed up against each person to bless them. (It was in contrast to the woman in the Bible who had to press through the crowds in order to touch the hem of Jesus' robe.) How gracious and merciful Jesus is.

After about five minutes of this silent worship, strong trembling took over my body and head, with my teeth chattering. I did not ask for this, or do anything to instigate it. Nearing the end of this protracted time of silence, I clearly heard the Holy Spirit say to me twice, *I am coming to visit My people, and this is preparation.* I was acutely aware that this was referring to The Church On The Way, although a number of other churches were represented in the audience. If God had spoken in an audible voice it could not have been more real, so I finally broke the silence by telling the audience exactly what God had said to me.

The Holy Spirit then directed me to invite anyone who had just experienced a vital encounter with the Lord to share it openly. This resulted in many meaningful testimonies, *all with depth of content.* These stories would be a chapter in itself. Many stated that it was truly a life-changing experience. All glory to the King. In addition, the following testimony from one who was at that retreat was sent to me in the mail.

Dear Joy,
I attended the singles' retreat in Big Bear and was delighted to hear you speak. I was

awed at the presence of the Lord among us.
When we experienced His manifest presence,
I felt His overwhelming largeness and power
and I thought, "I am not ready, and am not
worthy." After His greatness passed by, I saw it
recede and I thought, "He became small." But
then I realized that He was washing my feet.

And as He was lifting me, as if on a
pedestal, His eyes were scanning me from toe
to head, and in that scan I was being washed
and covered in glory. When He got to the top
of my head, it was as if to a child; He patted
my hair and kissed my forehead and turned
me to the world as if to say, "She is ready."

I felt the love of a bride at the altar and I
just smiled at so much love. He impressed me
with, "Therefore I do not condemn you, there is
no condemnation." I didn't know if this was for
everyone, or just for me, but I wanted to share
it with you.

I can report, from being personally involved many times in these kinds of gatherings, how wonderful they are. In fact, all the deepest moves of God's Spirit that I have been in have always been when God was given *time* to move without the usual constraints and restrictions.

The Body of Christ understands so little of the fear of the Lord and experiences so little of what it means to tremble in the presence of our awesome God. Could it be that we know so little of the discipline of silent focused worship? I often ponder with awe and wonder what thirty minutes of silent worship in heaven will be like, as described in Revelation. Also, while ever we are bound by our liturgy and traditions, God is restricted in releasing the outpouring of His Spirit upon us in deeper dimensions.

God longs to manifest Himself in far greater ways to His people. But He does not reward casual inquirers, only diligent seekers. When spiritual leaders are content with "church as usual," then that is exactly what we will get. And we get it far too frequently. In my book *The Fire of God*, I clearly outline the need to get out of our comfort zones into where God is really in charge. There is a world of difference.

While it is very important to obey God because of what He says, it is even more important to obey Him for who He is. In order for God to test us on this, He often tells us to do unusual things that seem to us illogical. In the next chapter, I share the fulfillment of obedience under those circumstances.

2

Obedience Because of Who God Is

The fear of God is directly connected with obedience. When Abraham was about to slay his son, Isaac, in obedience to the voice of the Lord, the angel said to him, "Now I know that you fear God, seeing you have not withheld your son, your only son, from me" (Genesis 22:12).

Often, I have heard sincere testimonies that go like this: "God spoke to me, but I did not obey. Then God spoke to me again. I did not obey." Or, "One week or one year later, God came and spoke to me again. I still did not obey." I have also heard, "Then, after a week of arguing with God, I finally gave in and said, 'Okay, God.'"

These testimonies reveal the lack of the fear of God.

When the mariners on board the ship that was going to Tarshish asked Jonah his occupation, where he had come from and his nationality, Jonah replied, "I am a Hebrew; and I fear the LORD, the God of heaven, who made the sea and the dry land" (Jonah 1:9). But his *lack of the fear of the*

Lord was vividly evident by his disobedience to God in not going to the city of Nineveh with the word of the Lord, and by his deliberately going in another direction!

However, the mariners manifested genuine fear of the Lord by their reactions to Jonah's testimony of disobedience, and his subsequent announcement that the terrible storm was an act of God on his account. Before throwing him overboard, at his suggestion, they cried to the Lord, "We beseech thee, O LORD, let us not perish for this man's life, and lay not on us innocent blood; for thou, O LORD, hast done as it pleased thee" (Jonah 1:14). Then afterward when the sea became immediately calm, "the men feared the LORD exceedingly, and they offered a sacrifice to the LORD and made vows" (Jonah 1:16).

Jonah had to learn through a series of horrifying experiences that the consequences of disobedience are always far harder than the act of obedience, no matter how hard! We always have God's grace given us to enable us to obey. We come under His judgment when we disobey.

After Jonah's repentance in the middle of the fish's stomach, God delivered him; and then Jonah manifested the genuine fear of the Lord through obedience in going to Nineveh with God's message.

Like all of us who repent of sin, we can then experience the truth of Psalm 130:3–4: "If thou, O LORD, shouldst mark iniquities, Lord, who could stand? But there is forgiveness with thee, that thou mayest be feared."

The more we take the time to study the character of God from His Word, facet by facet, the more He will reveal

Himself to us. The deeper the understanding that we have of His justice, knowledge, wisdom, faithfulness and love, the easier it will be for us to obey Him.

The fear of God is evidenced in our lives by *instant, joyful* and *whole* obedience to God. That is biblical obedience. Anything else is disobedience. Delayed obedience is disobedience. Partial obedience is disobedience. Doing what God has asked with murmuring is disobedience.

Do you know the two greatest incentives you and I can have to obey God? First, the knowledge of what He is really like; second, the fear of the Lord. The two go hand in hand.

There will be that first moment when we see Jesus face to face. What a moment!

We will see Him in all His dazzling beauty, majestic splendor, blazing glory, the fire of His purity and the depth of His unfathomable love. Oh, the wonder of it all as we look into the eyes of Him who is infinite in wisdom and knowledge.

We are going to have one of two reactions: We will react with shock if we have not been gazing at Him down here through His Word with a passionate, intense desire to know Him, and in faith, believing He will reveal Himself to us. And we are going to say, "Oh, You are like *that*?!" because we do not really know Him. Or, we will react by saying, "Oh, I knew You were like that! So I am not really too surprised, because You have already revealed much of Your beauty and glory to me. You rewarded me on earth with that revelation as I diligently sought to know You. You put the desire in my heart to spend hours alone with You, which ruined me for the ordinary. I knew You were as You are, but You are *so much more!*"

31

Is the latter going to be our reaction? It would not be a great big shock to Moses when he reached heaven. He had spent so much time with God on earth. God! Exciting, scintillating, fascinating, wonderful, beautiful, fabulous, precious, tender God! If Moses needed grace to go up on the mountain alone with God and stay there, he needed more grace to come down to be with the people!

As a teenager, I used to sing, "Absolutely tender, absolutely true, understanding all things, understanding You. Infinitely loving, exquisitely dear. This is God our Father, what have we to fear?"

Do we know Him? We will, if we take time to diligently seek Him. "He is a rewarder of them that diligently seek him" (Hebrews 11:6, KJV). Do we read the Bible to get messages out of the Bible to give to people, or do we read the Bible with the passionate desire to know the Author of the Book? When we see Him as He is in all His blazing glory, majestic splendor and awesome holiness, that revelation becomes the greatest motivation to obey Him instantly, joyfully and wholly. It becomes a preposterous thought *not* to obey Him!

God wants to bring us to the place where *what* He tells us to do is not nearly as important as *who* He is who gives the order. When we put the emphasis on the "what" and not the "who," we have things in the wrong perspective.

When Jesus was on earth, He never placed any more importance on raising the dead than on blessing a child. He never started a denomination on either event! The important thing to Him was that the Father had given an order, and it was the Son's delight to carry it out.

32

Many times, God tests us by telling us to do things without our having the faintest idea why we are to do them. We do not need to understand why. We need to understand *who He is*, who is speaking. *He, God*, in His infinite knowledge and wisdom, knows why—that is good enough reason for us, with our finite knowledge and wisdom, to obey.

Abraham could probably have written a book on the reasons why he should not be sacrificing Isaac on an altar, according to his own human reasoning and desires, but he hated the sin of disobedience to God more than he loved his only son. He passed the test, and proved by doing so the deep level of the fear of God operating in his life. He also exercised great faith by believing God to raise Isaac from the dead, in order for God's promises to be fulfilled through him (see Hebrews 11:19).

One time when I was in Lausanne, Switzerland, teaching twice daily at Youth With a Mission's School of Evangelism, I was downtown in the afternoon doing some shopping in a department store. I was not looking for clothing, but I noticed a large table with clothing on it and saw that the garments were at sale price. I soon found a smart dress, exactly my size, good quality, at a very reasonable price, and my interest was aroused. What woman's interest would not be? But I quickly remembered I had a brand-new dress with me that was very similar. Also, I had other countries on my itinerary, and my luggage was already overweight. I did not need the dress, and I did not have excess money to spend on it anyway. However, I had a strong impression to go into the fitting room and try it on. It was perfect. I loved it. But it made no sense to buy it.

I had long since learned to seek the Lord about matters small and large in my life, and I knew obedience to Him was where the action was. So, I slowly and deliberately died out, with an act of my will, to all human reasoning and desire on the basis of Proverbs 3:5, "Do not rely on your own insight," and Proverbs 28:26, "He who trusts in his own mind is a fool," and Luke 22:42, "Not my will, but thine, be done."

Then, I took authority over Satan and demon powers and resisted them and silenced them in the name of the Lord Jesus Christ according to James 4:7, "Resist the devil and he will flee from you." So they could not speak to me.

I then thanked God that according to John 10:3–4, 27, where He says His sheep hear His voice, know His voice and follow Him; and according to Psalm 32:8, "I will instruct you and teach you the way you should go; I will counsel you with my eye upon you," He would tell me what to do.

Very clearly, He repeatedly told me I was to buy it. I well remember saying to Him, "Because of the fear of the Lord that is upon me, I obey You." I then bought the dress.

Two days later, I said to the Lord, "Well, I obeyed You over that dress, but I still have no understanding why You should want me to have two almost identical dresses on this trip. Could You please give me understanding?"

He then said, "You are to give away the other new one to one of the students and keep this one for yourself." I was thrilled at the thought of being used as a steward to meet another's need, but there were many students, and I did not have a clue which was the right one. As I asked Him which one, He brought before me the face of one of the girls. I did not know her name.

I said, "If this impression is correct, then please confirm it to me in some way."

This was a Saturday morning and the majority of the students had gone away for the day. A short time later I answered a knock at my bedroom door, and there in front of me was the exact student whose face had come before me in prayer. She was embarrassed and hesitant at disturbing me, and said, "I really do not understand this at all, but I believe the Lord has shown me I'm to come to you and give you this simple little bookmark I made some months ago. I have no idea why He should tell me to do this, but I do know I want to obey Him."

She obviously had the fear of God upon her.

I said, "Come on in, honey. I know why you're here. I have a story that will blow your little mind."

When I had finished, she put on the dress and, of course, it was perfect in every way for her; and we squealed with delight! Then she told me her story.

I had been teaching during the week on the fear of the Lord, obedience and seeking God with all our hearts to know Him; and she had decided to spend her day off putting some of it into practice.

As she was reading her Bible and asking God to reveal Himself to her, she started thinking of her need for a new dress. She had no money to buy one. She dismissed those thoughts and started telling God she wanted to know Him more than anything else. She said, "Have You anything to say to me?" An impression immediately came to her mind, *Matthew 6:25.* She could not remember what it was about, but she looked it up. It was the start of Jesus' discourse about providing us with food and clothing when we put His righteousness and His interests first. She worshiped God for this direct, intimate conversation, via His Word, and *went on seeking Him.* A little while later, she asked again if there was anything else He wanted to say to her. He quietly spoke again into her mind, *Luke 12:28.* Again she had no remembrance of what the verse was, but she looked it up and found, "But if God so clothes the grass which is alive in the field today and tomorrow is thrown into the oven, how much more will he clothe you, O men of little faith!" She read in verse 31, "Seek his kingdom, and these things shall be yours as well." She continued to read, pray and praise. Then He told her to go and give me the worn bookmark with *no* understanding why.

As I read the two verses she had written on it, I knew why; they were of tremendous encouragement to me as I was away from my home and family at the clear call of God for three-and-a-half months at that time, teaching the Word of God in many nations: 1 Corinthians 15:58, "Be steadfast, immovable, always abounding in the work of the Lord, knowing that in the Lord your labor is not in vain," and 1 Thessalonians 5:24, "He who calls you is faithful, and he will do it."

This story comes out of simple, everyday circumstances that are engineered by God to test His children on the fear of the Lord.

When we have it—we obey.

When we do not—we do our own thing and miss an exciting, intimate relationship with God and the blessings that go with it.

One of the students from that same school has since become a Bible teacher who teaches on the fear of the Lord. He also teaches it to his own children with remarkable results. He wrote me the following testimony (the names have been changed):

The Lord led me to speak to the International Christian School parents on the fear of the Lord. As I spoke, I realized that the fear of the Lord results in all we want our children to learn—total obedience, 100 percent truth, no murmuring or complaining, release from the fear of man, and answers in the area of relationships.

So the next morning in our family devotions I prayed that they might learn to fear the Lord: to learn to hate sin as He hates it; to hate the sin of not telling the truth; to hate the sin of disobedience, murmuring, complaining, and so on. For two weeks in family devotions, I did that every day. Usually when I go away, Kay has a rather difficult time with the boys and I am met at the airport with a series of negative reports. So before taking a trip, and after two weeks of doing this, I sat the boys down and asked, "What do I expect from you while I am gone?"

"To obey Mommy, of course," they replied.

I said, "Okay, turn to her and promise her that"—which they did. Then I said, "Now I want you to tell the Lord, 'We promise to obey Mommy while Daddy is gone, and if we don't do it we want You to discipline us!'"

Greg (eight years old) immediately responded, "No way!" Of course, I was very encouraged because I saw he *was* learning the fear of the Lord (at least he did not want to lie). Well, after a few minutes of further explanation and encouragement he agreed; so did Brian (four years old).

When I returned from three weeks of ministry, they had *never* had such a fantastic time while I was away! One day Kay woke up sick, and when Brian saw her condition, he told her he was going to be her servant the whole day. And that is just exactly what he did.

I continued praying this prayer each day for three more weeks, and then I went on a three-week trip again. Upon my return an even more fantastic report followed! So the fear of the Lord has become a part of our regular family devotions; the boys even place their hands on my hand now as an agreement with me in prayer.

One morning I had just done this and sat down, when I heard the following prayer from my four-year-old: "Dear Jesus, teach Daddy to fear You that he might learn to hate sin as You do, too." Praise the Lord!

We may well be thinking, *If there were only God and myself, it would be relatively easy to manifest the fear of the Lord; but when a lot of others are involved—it's tough.*

But God wants to see whose approval we are really living for—His or others.

It was in the seventies and early eighties when Loren Cunningham, Campbell McAlpine and I were teamed together at God's direction to speak at numbers of spiritual leadership conferences across America. At the time of the following story, we were in Chattanooga, Tennessee. As was our custom, we met for all of the day before the conference to pray for God to move mightily during the rest of the week.

It was on that Sunday evening that we were directed by the Holy Spirit to phone Youth With a Mission's base in Georgia and invite our staff and Discipleship Training School students to drive through from Georgia and attend the conference the next day. They took those last-minute challenges admirably, and arrived for the evening meeting the next day.

After I had spoken on the fear of the Lord, a young black man from that school asked if he could speak with me privately. He shared that he had problems with impure thoughts related to women and had been asking God to help him overcome them. God answered him in a vivid dream. He saw me in a long white dress, speaking to an audience, and God said clearly, "She will give you the help you need." He had never met me, and had no way that he knew of to meet me. But when I got up to speak, he instantly recognized me as the one he had seen in the dream. He marveled at God's faithfulness and ways, and acknowledged that his prayers were being fully answered. I taught on the truths that are presented in this book.

When I first started to speak on a series of messages on the fear of the Lord at that conference, and had only given the first three points, which took about twenty minutes, I said, "Sometimes God tests us in unusual ways to see whether we will obey Him for who He is." Immediately I heard the Holy Spirit say to me, *Sit down and don't teach another word.* I reported to the congregation what I had heard and promptly sat down without another word.

The chairman of the conference got up and talked, without saying anything of any consequence, and sat down. Then Campbell McAlpine, a well-known Bible teacher from England, walked forward from where he had been sitting with Loren Cunningham and took the microphone. In obedience to the Holy Spirit, he led the congregation in application of the points I had just shared.

He asked the people to be starkly honest and repent before God where they had not been living the teaching I had just given. He called them to openly share anything in relation to that conviction, as prompted by the Holy Spirit. For the next hour or more (not less), many spiritual leaders stood and acknowledged with genuine brokenness before God where they had not feared the Lord in the areas just taught. There were many in tears and some were prostrate on the floor in deep repentance. The Holy Spirit invaded that conference room and brought radical changes in people's lives.

When we genuinely fear the Lord, we will obey Him instantly, wholly and joyfully, because of who He is. We are unimpressed with men's reactions to our actions—only impressed with God's reactions to our actions.

I can remember thinking that day, as I obeyed God's simple instructions to me, *This is Your conference, not mine. These are Your people, not mine. This is Your agenda, not mine. These are Your truths, not mine. These are Your instructions, not mine. Therefore the outcome is Your responsibility, not mine, including receiving all the glory.* I sat there in perfect peace, watching God working mightily in front of my eyes.

The next day, as I continued teaching the truths that are in this book, God broke through in a more awesome way. After I had been teaching for about an hour, again, Campbell McAlpine walked forward and took the microphone. He had received impressions, which he had submitted to Loren Cunningham, who, after seeking God, confirmed they were from the Holy Spirit.

Campbell explained to the people that in his daily Bible reading that morning, he had observed for the first time that, straight after Mary of Bethany had poured the expensive perfume over Jesus, Judas had criticized her lavish act of devotion to the Master. Campbell then stated that the Holy Spirit had revealed to him that there was a "Judas" in the conference who was critical of the message and the messenger whom God was using to bring this teaching on the fear of God, because she was a woman.

Campbell continued to speak with the authority that comes from being a humble, holy prophet of God, full of the Holy Spirit and the fear of the Lord. He simply said, "Stand up whoever you are, and openly acknowledge that you are the Judas. Repent, and we will pray for God's mercy to be released to you." The silence was deafening. You could have heard a feather fall on a velvet cushion. The sense of the fear of God was palpable.

The awesome silence continued—at length! Campbell remained standing in quiet, unshakable faith that it was God's responsibility to complete the work that He alone had started. At least ten minutes elapsed—probably more.

Finally a well-dressed, well-educated, good-looking man, a highly respected deacon (or elder) in his church, stood to his feet and with a loud voice said, "I am the Judas, and I don't want my bowels to drop out." He went on to explain that he had been resisting the Holy Spirit's conviction, because of the high standard of truth I was sharing—particularly from my teaching in Psalm 34:11–13. I had been emphasizing that the first lesson in God's school on the fear of the Lord is that we must have "lips free from deceit." That means we must only speak 100 percent truth, 100 percent of the time. I followed by illustrating how that works in everyday conversations. I share some of them in chapter 14.

That dear man deeply repented of his resistance to God and to me and humbled himself before God and man. He openly asked for my forgiveness, which was fully given him. Campbell led out in a powerful prayer for the release of God's mercy toward him. The whole congregation joined in with fervency and faith, with their hearts and hands outstretched toward the man.

On the last day of that historic conference, that humble lawyer came to me privately to show the genuineness of his repentance. In a prayer, he vowed before God, and with me as a witness on earth, that never again as a lawyer would he ever say anything but 100 percent truth. He explained that this could mean losing or jeopardizing the success of his practice and the means of his livelihood. He had a wife and several children to support.

Lawyers are paid to defend their clients under all circumstances. Whether they state the truth or tell lies is irrelevant.

When I laid my hands on him and prayed that he would be saturated with the fear of the Lord, which means to hate the sin of lying (Proverbs 8:13), he and I knew that as we received this request by faith, God was actually impregnating his whole being with the fear of the Lord. God's manifest presence was very strong. I will never forget it.

Years later, the chairman of that conference mailed me a full-page article from the leading newspaper in Chattanooga. The whole subject in writing and in pictures was greatly honoring this exact same man. He had just been appointed as a judge.

> He who conceals his transgressions will not prosper, but he who confesses and forsakes them will obtain mercy.
>
> Proverbs 28:13

> Humble yourselves therefore under the mighty hand of God, that in due time he may exalt you.
>
> 1 Peter 5:6

> He who fears God shall come forth from them all.
>
> Ecclesiastes 7:18

The next chapter further illustrates how God sets up unusual and difficult circumstances and how we can come through smiling and without sweating!

3

Release from the Fear of Man

The fear of the Lord is the *only* way to be released from the fear of man.

Every honest person has to admit that he or she has been plagued by the fear of man at some stage in his or her life and has proved the truth from God's Word that it brings a snare (see Proverbs 29:25).

The fear of man is being more impressed with man's reaction to our actions than with God's reaction. That is bondage. When we have the fear of God upon us, we are impressed *only* with God's reaction. We are freed from the concern of what people think. That is freedom! That is release! That is great relief!

We do not necessarily get there overnight, but we do get there! One way is by constantly sending short telegram prayers to God, like, "I've heard what *they* think, what do *You* think?" and then acting according to His revealed opinion—regardless of the consequences. The more God-conscious we are, the less self-conscious we are. The more concern we have for God's approval in every situation, the more confidence He releases to us to act with His authority.

God often tests us in this area of the fear of people versus the fear of the Lord. But the test will always be to the level of our sincerity to want it, our present experience in it and our knowledge of the character of God. God, in His infinite wisdom and understanding, will not test us beyond the knowledge we have to be able to pass the test. He is just, gentle, wise and unswervingly faithful, and He tests us accordingly. He will test us in small circumstances first, then increasingly in circumstances of greater consequence as we keep operating in the fear of the Lord. I had been tested on the fear of the Lord over many years and in many ways before He allowed me the privilege of the following experience.

In August of 1980, I was speaking each day for a week at a retreat at Christ For The Nations Institute in Dallas, Texas. On Thursday afternoon, I had been teaching on a radio program in the Dallas area for two hours. Thursday evening was the first opportunity I had to seek God at length for understanding as to what message He wanted me to give to the people the next day. I received nothing, so I finally went to bed.

Early on Friday morning, I sought God again for many hours, and still received no direction from God as to the word of the Lord. The meeting was scheduled for 10:45 A.M.

Isaiah 50:10 was quickened to me several times but without any understanding: "Who among you fears the LORD and obeys the voice of his servant, who walks in darkness and has no light, yet trusts in the name of the LORD and relies upon his God?"

I went to the meeting, taking my briefcase with all my notebooks that contain the many messages God has given me over the years, although twice when I was getting ready I had an impression come to my mind that all I was going to need was my Bible.

When I arrived on the platform, I explained to Mrs. Freda Lindsay, the chairwoman of the meeting, that although I had sought God earnestly for many hours concerning the message, He had not yet released it to me. Until He did, I had nothing to say! She announced this to the audience, graciously saying she trusted the Lord in me fully, and she called several people in spiritual leadership up to the platform to join with her in faith as she prayed over me for God to release the message. She also invited the audience to stand and to believe God with her. They all did. I stood thanking God silently that He would tell me what to speak on, as I had done many times before, in relation to that service.

When my dear sister Freda had finished praying, and when the others had left the platform, still there was only silence from heaven. I stood alone listening, trusting and counting on His faithfulness, for between five and ten minutes, conscious only of the fear of God. I asked God to speak to me from His Word. I opened my Bible and immediately my eyes fell on Isaiah 50:10, "Who among you fears the LORD and obeys the voice of his servant, who walks in darkness and has no light, yet trusts in the name of the LORD and relies upon his God?" Only then did I understand this was primarily a test from God related to the fear of the Lord and that it was also a demonstration of it to the people. (I was later told by people in the audience that the fear of the Lord permeated the whole place.) Still there was no direction as to what to speak on, so I continued to wait upon God. More minutes passed.

Finally, I heard God say to me, *Read Jeremiah 6.* In that instance, I knew three things:

1. I had received some direction from Him.
2. I would obey Him.
3. I had no message on Jeremiah 6!

I invited the people to turn to Jeremiah 6, explaining that God had just told me to read it to them. I read it. I waited on God again. More minutes passed, then He clearly spoke into my mind, *Read verses ten and nineteen again. I am going to speak through you on these verses.* I did, and He did.

Verse 10 says, "To whom shall I speak and give warning, that they may hear? Behold, their ears are closed, they cannot listen; behold, the word of the LORD is to them an object of scorn, they take no pleasure in it." Verse 19 says, "Hear, O earth; behold, I am bringing evil upon this people, the fruit of their devices, because they have not given heed to my words; and as for my law, they have rejected it."

God spoke through me spontaneously that morning on what it means to disobey the word of the Lord when He brings it through His servants, and on what it means to reject His Word. We only have to neglect it to do that! Both are symptoms of the lack of the fear of God. "I am a companion of all who fear thee, of those who keep thy precepts" (Psalm 119:63).

Earlier that week, I had arranged to have lunch with a man, his wife and his daughter for that particular Friday lunchtime after my message. He was on the pastoral staff of Christ For The Nations at that time. He was not at that meeting where I had spoken, and he knew nothing about what had taken place. Over the lunch table, he handed me a piece of paper with a verse of Scripture written out and said, "Yesterday God strongly impressed upon me that I was to give you this verse today." It was Psalm 31:19: "O how abundant is thy goodness, which thou hast laid up for those who fear thee, and wrought for those who take refuge in thee, in the sight of the sons of men!"

After praising God for this promise and thanking this brother for his sensitivity to God on my behalf, I then told him what had just taken place that made the verse so relevant and meaningful to me. We were both greatly encouraged in the Lord.

On another occasion, I was tested by God in a similar way. I was on the island of Cyprus during the week of September 29 through October 2, 1981, speaking at a spiritual leadership conference. Leaders had come from different parts of the Middle East representing different missionary organizations. I had already spoken on Tuesday morning, the 29th, and was scheduled to speak again in the evening of that day.

Throughout the afternoon, I earnestly sought the Lord for the evening message, but received no direction from Him.

In the late afternoon, I shared this with the leader of the conference, and we both sought God together to see if there was any other plan He wanted to reveal to us. We both received strong scriptural guidance that I was to speak. I continued seeking God right up until the time to start the meeting at 7:30 P.M., and still I received no direction or understanding. At 8:00 P.M., the leader announced that I would speak. I, in turn, told the people I had no message as yet, and asked them to pray that God would release it to me, which they did.

At 8:45 P.M., I still had absolutely no direction whatsoever. But I explained to the people that God's plan and way are always perfect and that He was obviously trying to teach us some new things as a group; I urged them to keep looking to Him, resting in Him, and trusting Him for the release of the word of the Lord.

At ten minutes past nine—one hour and ten minutes after the meeting had been handed over to me—the Lord directed my thoughts to Lamentations 3:25–26: "The LORD is good to those who wait for him, to the soul that seeks him. It is good that one should wait quietly for the salvation of the LORD."

These Scriptures were quickened to me with the clear understanding that I was to speak briefly on "Waiting on God" and that I was to share two other stories out of my life where God tested me in relation to waiting at length for His direction during times of pressure.

God has His sovereign way of teaching, by testing a leader in front of the people. When we fear God, we pass the test, and the people learn the ways of God. If in this case the teacher had failed the test, the people would have been denied "the word of the Lord," and the speaker would have proved to God that she still feared men.

It can cost us many things to fear God and not men—being misunderstood, the loss of friendships, closed doors in ministry, rejection of many kinds, persecution and even life itself.

It cost Zechariah and Stephen their lives to say what God told them to say. They feared God, not the people. The prophets Jeremiah, Micaiah and Hanani were all imprisoned for giving the word of the Lord. They feared God, not the people. Paul, Silas and Peter were imprisoned for aggressively witnessing for Jesus Christ. They feared God, not the people.

It is possible to have enough of the fear of God upon us to give the word of the Lord to the people with real authority and then to succumb to the fear of man after having given it. Jotham is an example of this in Judges 9:7–21. After speaking with great boldness on the top of Mount Gerizim in bringing rebuke and challenge, we then read, "And Jotham ran away and fled, and went to Beer and dwelt there, for fear of Abimelech his brother" (verse 21).

In 1 Kings 18 and 19, we find Elijah doing the same thing. After challenging the nation of Israel, plus hundreds of the prophets of Baal and Asherah with dramatic boldness on Mount Carmel, we find him running away in fear after 28 threatening words from one woman—Jezebel.

The Lord Jesus said in Luke 12:4–5, "I tell you, my friends, do not fear those who kill the body, and after that have no more that they can do. But I will warn you whom to fear:

fear him who, after he has killed, has power to cast into hell; yes, I tell you, fear him!"

Whenever there is pressure from men's opinions, weigh each decision in the light of the judgment seat of Christ, where each one of us shall give account of himself to God (see Romans 14:12). Then it is not hard to obey God in a difficult situation. It costs us so much more when we fear men and not God. It costs us the privilege and joy of intimacy of friendship with God. What a price!

God releases true authority in ministry only to those who are more impressed with His reactions to their actions than with men's reactions to their actions. This is what marked Jesus as unique among the other teachers of His day. "And when Jesus finished these sayings, the crowds were astonished at his teaching, for he taught them as one who had authority, and not as their scribes" (Matthew 7:28–29).

The Lord Jesus lived on this earth as Son of Man, putting aside His function of deity, while retaining His nature of deity.

He never acted independently of His Father God. He lived in total submission, availability, dependence, obedience and faith. "Jesus said to them, 'Truly, truly, I say to you, the Son can do nothing of his own accord, but only what he sees the Father doing; for whatever he does, that the Son does likewise'" (John 5:19). The Father was the explanation of what took place in the life of the Lord Jesus. As a result, everything He said and did was with authority.

Jesus said, "As the Father has sent me, even so I send you" (John 20:21).

Our ministries are marked with authority only to the degree that the life of the Lord Jesus is the only explanation of what comes forth from us. This is possible as we consciously, willfully lean on the Person of the Lord Jesus Christ in faith to do in us and through us what we are totally convinced we cannot do ourselves. We simply say, "I can't, but You can, and will now. Thank You," and take the next step of obedience. His supernatural life is then released according to our need.

We cannot believe that God will speak through us with authority unless we have first of all been sent by God to speak. "For he whom God has sent utters the words of God, for it is not by measure that he gives the Spirit" (John 3:34).

Anyone with a natural ability to communicate can speak with liberty, but not necessarily have any spiritual authority. Authority from God is released only to those whose activity originates from God and is energized by Him. Then and then only can God receive the glory. Jesus said, "I have brought you glory on earth by completing the work you gave me to do" (John 17:4, NIV). We have no spiritual authority outside obedience to God.

Many times people confuse forceful speaking and eloquence, even when truth is being conveyed, with spiritual authority. Only what is spoken with God's authority will touch men's spirits and motivate them to take the necessary steps of obedience that will change their lives. All else touches only the intellect and/or the emotions.

A few stammered words spoken with authority will pierce men's hearts, more than a thousand sermons delivered without authority, though they are homiletically correct. If God prompts us to weep, and say nothing, then when we weep we will weep with authority. And God will make it known to the people that the weeping originated from Him and was energized by Him.

The Scottish preacher Murray McCheyne got up to preach one Sunday morning and in obedience to God all he could do was weep. This resulted in a mighty move of God's Spirit upon the people, who in turn were broken before the Lord in repentance. He was experiencing Paul's testimony, "We are not trying to please men but God, who tests our hearts" (1 Thessalonians 2:4, NIV).

Only the right person at the right place at the right time, in the right condition of heart toward God and men, saying and doing the right things, can believe God for the right results. It takes time to seek God to make sure these conditions are fulfilled. But the reward is a life of coordination and fulfillment.

It is twenty years since *Intimate Friendship with God* was first published, where I shared stories about God testing me on the fear of God versus the fear of men. The story I am going to share took place less than two years ago. I can only assume that God wanted to have an up-to-date testimony for this new edition.

I had received a phone call from Pastor Benny Hinn's secretary, inviting me to come to his studio in four days time for a TV interview related to my book *The Fire of God*, which had recently been published. The invitation included joining him afterward to attend his Monday evening Bible class, where he taught several hundred people who came for an eight-week course of in-depth teaching.

I responded by saying that Jim and I would seek God and get His answer back to her as soon as possible. When we waited on God, having died out to our human reasonings and desires, and resisted the enemy's voice in Jesus' name, we both had impressions that I was to accept, accompanied by God's peace.

The next day, we sought again specifically to know if God had a purpose for us to attend Pastor Benny's teaching class. We did not want to presume anything. The Holy Spirit's answer to us both was "yes." To me, the additional words, "It is important," were clearly spoken into my spirit.

From many years of having the great privilege of being linked with Pastor Benny in ministry assignments, I have learned to be prepared for the unexpected and the unusual. So the next day I sought God diligently to know what God would have me share from His Word, should Benny spontaneously ask me to do so. This had happened on previous occasions!

As a result of my waiting on God, everywhere I turned in my Bible, verses on the control of the tongue and the importance of our words were standing out and being quickened to me by the Holy Spirit. Because of severe time constraints, all I could do was to find the message I had recently worked on and given on the implications of our words and how they shape our destinies. I put the big notebook in my bag and took it with me, wondering how in the world this lengthy new message would ever work with Benny's program—and why?

The next day we taped the TV interview at his studios. That evening, we arrived at the packed-out Bible class, with Pastor Benny announcing our arrival and saying, "I know Joy Dawson has something to share with us this evening. Come and sit right up here at the front, Joy and Jim." We did.

Pastor Benny was speaking under a strong anointing, a very powerful message on the blood of the Lord Jesus and how it should be applied to every area of our lives. The more he taught, the more I wondered what on earth the word of the Lord about the tongue had to do with what he was teaching.

I asked God to confirm to me from His Word if I was still to share with this audience about the importance of our words. When I opened my Bible, I found it was at Matthew 12 and my eyes immediately fell on verses 36 and 37. They were some of the exact same verses God had spoken to me from the night before. "But I say to you that for every idle word men may speak, they will give account of it in the day of judgment. For by your words you will be justified, and by your words you will be condemned" (NKJV).

I was extremely thankful that I had done my homework, to be somewhat prepared in case this scenario eventuated. But I didn't have a clue how much *time* I was going to be given to share, or *what* I was to share from this hour and a half of teaching material I had. Was I just to start at the beginning?

I distinctly remember repeatedly thinking that everything about my situation was insane in the natural reasoning. Here I was, seated right under the speaker's nose on the front row with my large teaching notebook, not taking notes, but seeking God as if my life depended on it. "Where do I *start* in this message, Lord?" I inquired (interspersed with fervent, whispered requests to Jim to pray for wisdom and direction to be given me). Finally, I received clear direction from the Holy Spirit where I was to start. It was somewhere in the middle of my notes. That direction brought tremendous relief—believe me.

At the end of two hours of teaching, Pastor Benny simply said, "Now Joy Dawson will come and *pray*" (not speak). What was I to do? Do the only logical thing, and what appeared to be the only right thing, by doing only what I was asked to do? Fear man and disobey God's clear directions, or fear God and follow through in obedience to that voice that has led me throughout my long lifetime?

I went to the platform with my awkward-looking big notebook in hand, stood by my dear friend Benny and said to him, "I'm so glad we really know each other as friends after all these years, because I need to ask you if you would release me to share what God has spoken to me from His Word in relation to this class." Benny said, "Yes, you may." I taught for about five minutes on the link between the fear of God and the words we speak. I showed the emphasis God's Word places on the evidences of the fear of the Lord operating in a person's life. It is to the degree that person speaks 100 percent of the truth 100 percent of the time. I read from Psalm 34:11–13 where the first lesson on the fear of the Lord is related to having our "lips free from deceit." I said that God has a lot to say in His Word about the sin of deceit. Deceit manifests itself in overstatement or understatement. By adding a few words or leaving a few words out we can distort the truth. In failing to report the setting or the context in which the words were spoken, we can give a distortion of truth. The words spoken could have been in humor.

Our standard for living and speaking is the life of the Lord Jesus. When describing Jesus as our example, 1 Peter 2:21–22 says, "that you should follow His steps: 'Who committed no sin, nor was deceit found in His mouth'" (NKJV). Also, Revelation 14:5 says, "In their mouth was found no deceit, for they are without fault before the throne of God" (NKJV).

At that point Pastor Benny said, "I think you should stop now, Joy. But I want you to come back and be the guest speaker at the banquet we are having at the close of this school. I want you to speak from your new book *The Fire of God*." I felt complete peace with Benny's leadership instructions. I believe I had shared exactly what God wanted me to say, and that dear Benny had been given a clear signal from the Holy Spirit to say what he did. I replied that I would seek the Lord about Benny's invitation, and immediately did. Before he had finished closing the meeting in prayer, God had answered me with the words, *Yes, I have opened this door.* So I committed myself publicly by accepting the invitation as I shared what God had spoken. Then Benny greatly encouraged me by announcing that he was giving a copy of my book *The Fire of God* to the four hundred class members, as a gift.

The sequel to all this is that at the class banquet, after I had spoken on the preparation and price for revival (which is part of *The Fire of God*), a man came and spoke to me privately. He said he had been a Christian for many years and was a practicing lawyer of many years. But when I spoke following Benny Hinn's teaching at the Bible class about the importance and implications of our words and quoted the Scriptures related to that subject, he had a totally life-changing experience. He kept repeating, "I will never be the same." He conveyed with deep conviction that the Holy Spirit had powerfully impacted his life in those five minutes. He said, "I cannot thank you enough for your obedience to say exactly what I needed to hear. Thank you. Thank you."

Wow! Can you imagine what that kind of encouragement brought to me? I never had the opportunity to explain to him what testing I had gone through to be the instrument to bless him in such a profound way. But I was deeply grateful for his sharing his testimony.

Some weeks later I was sitting in my home church, The Church On The Way, in Van Nuys, California. It was at the end of a Wednesday evening prayer service, and I was waiting for the executive pastor to come and have the arranged appointment with me.

A young woman came to me and started to share how God had significantly spoken to her when I had briefly shared about the fear of the Lord and the words we speak at the Benny Hinn Bible class (a ninety-minute drive away). The pastor arrived just as she was speaking to me, terminating her account. I would love to have heard more. But it was enough for God to assure me that He was working out His purposes in the lives of others through my times of testing.

When we obey God because of the fear of the Lord upon our lives, we can take great comfort in the promises He has given to bless us. The following are just two of many.

> The LORD takes pleasure in those who fear Him, in those who hope in His mercy.
>
> Psalm 147:11, NKJV

> The friendship of the LORD is for those who fear him, and he makes known to them his covenant.
>
> Psalm 25:14

Every time we choose to fear God and not men, we can be assured that we have brought God pleasure, and that He will bring us into closer fellowship with Himself, and that He will reveal the secrets from His Word to us. Wow! What rewards!

To the degree we choose to live in submission, availability, dependence, obedience and faith to the Lord Jesus, He will release His authority to us in the same way the Father did to the Son.

It is worth all the learning, the difficulties, the tests that are inevitable in developing our friendship with God, when we begin to realize that He is the most exciting Person in the universe, as well as the most holy. With this in mind, let us have a look now at this aspect of Him.

4

The Importance of God's Holiness

I believe the most important part of God's character is His holiness.

We will never understand the mercy of God until we have understood the holiness of God. (Mercy is not getting the punishment we deserve.) We will never understand the wrath of God in His judgment on sin until we have understood the holiness of God. We will never understand the unfathomable depths of His love . . .

> that He could leave heaven's glory where He lived in unclouded communion with the Father from before time began;
>
> that He should come and live on this earth and be in the environment of sin;
>
> that He should take upon Himself the accumulative filth of the sins of the world upon the cross

. . . until we have understood the holiness of God. "For our sake he made him to be sin who knew no sin, so that in him we might become the righteousness of God" (2 Corinthians 5:21). We will never understand the depth of the atonement—what it cost a holy God to manifest that kind of love—until we have understood the holiness of God.

The first reason holiness is the most important part of God's character is because of what is going on in heaven.

What was it that the seraphim surrounding the throne of God were crying out when Isaiah saw the Lord in that vision God gave him? "Holy, holy, holy is the LORD of hosts; the whole earth is full of his glory" (Isaiah 6:3).

What is it in Revelation 4:8 about which the four living creatures never cease to sing? It is not, "Great, great, great is God"; it is not, "Just, just, just is God"; it is not, "Loving, loving, loving is God." Those attributes of God are wonderful and very important! Yet God has chosen in His sovereignty that day and night living creatures are singing without ceasing, "Holy, holy, holy, is the Lord God Almighty, who was and is and is to come!" It is, therefore, of the utmost significance that we understand why.

It must be that God in His infinite wisdom and knowledge sees holiness as the attribute above every other of His attributes of which all heaven and earth need to be constantly reminded.

How important it must be! Have we taken time to study this part of God's character? Have we ever given one hour, one morning, one afternoon, one evening, or one day of our lives, uninterrupted, where we have said, "God, I am going to make a study of Your holiness from Your Word. I want to know You"?

The second reason is that the very name of the third Person of the Trinity, who is equal in authority though different in function, is named the *Holy* Spirit—not the Great Spirit, the Loving Spirit, nor the Wise Spirit, but the Holy Spirit.

The third reason is that His holiness is the basis of our respect for God, and therefore the main reason for our being able to commit ourselves totally to Him, in love and trust. We would be foolish to commit ourselves to someone when we did not have understanding of the righteousness of his character, regardless of his accomplishments or strength of personality.

The degree of our understanding of God's holiness will also determine the height and depth of our worship to Him. The greatest times of worship I have experienced have always occurred when I have focused my attention on God's awesome holiness. The revelation of the dazzling beauty of the Lord Jesus most often comes to those who have a passionate desire to see His holiness. "Strive for . . . holiness without which no one will see the Lord" (Hebrews 12:14). "For the LORD is righteous, he loves righteous deeds; the upright shall behold his face" (Psalm 11:7).

The beauty of the Lord Jesus comes from His holiness. When we gaze into the eyes of the Son of God, we see His eyes burn with the fire of His holiness and with the fire of His love. Do you know what that does to us? It ruins us for the ordinary. But that revelation is not given to the casual inquirer, only the diligent seeker.

Here are some of the reasons why the Son of God came to this earth:

1. to show us what the Father is like
2. to die upon the cross to make atonement for the sins of the world
3. to defeat the powers of darkness by His death and resurrection
4. to show us how to live
5. to become our life

I am so thankful that He came to show us how to live, because as I studied this aspect of His ministry on earth in Scripture, I found the standard Jesus Christ had in relation to the fear of God. Isaiah 11:2–3 says, "And the Spirit of the LORD shall rest upon him, the spirit of wisdom and understanding, the spirit of counsel and might, the spirit of knowledge and *the fear of the LORD. And his delight shall be in the fear of the LORD*" (italics added).

Jesus Christ, as Son of Man, chose continually to delight in holiness of thought, word and deed. He did not say, "In order to please My Father I will have to do this." Instead, He said, "I delight to choose the fear of God; I want holiness with intense desire."

Do we? Jesus' standard as the Son of Man is the standard we are to take when we realize He came to show us how to live.

In Proverbs 23:17 we read, "Continue in the fear of the LORD all the day." What does this mean? It means to choose holiness in our thoughts, in our words and in our deeds. The fear of the Lord should govern every part of our being.

The top priority that God Himself places on the fear of the Lord is found in Deuteronomy 10:12–13: "And now, Israel, what does the LORD your God require of you, but to fear the LORD your God . . . ?" This is before anything else. Then, He goes on to say, ". . . to walk in all his ways, to love him, to serve the LORD your God with all your heart and with all your soul, and to keep the commandments and statutes of the LORD, which I command you this day for your good."

Let us be honest now and take a look at how holy we are according to our attitudes about and reactions to sin. This next chapter can be very revealing!

5

Different Levels in Our Attitude toward Sin

There are four distinct levels of attitudes toward sin. An honest assessment will show us which level we are on and the need for application of the truths we are studying.

> Level One: The person who does not sin because the consequences are too great. This person lusts after someone else in his or her heart but does not commit the sin of adultery or fornication with his or her body because of the consequences being too great. Or he may hate someone else and wish that person were dead, but does not murder him because of the consequences. Obviously, there is no hatred of evil and, therefore, no fear of the Lord.
>
> Level Two: The person who lives by the Golden Rule. He wants peace at any price and cannot understand anyone who is so radical that he would try to change the status

quo of his life or anyone else's. This person can be full of the sins of selfishness and self-righteousness without being aware of it. He may go to church regularly every Sunday and give his tithes, pay his bills, grow six cabbages and give one over the fence to his neighbor. He often does good deeds. If you came up to him and said, "Do you fear the Lord?" he would be most indignant that you would even ask such a question of him. "Of course," he would reply. In fact, the "of course" could mean, "How could you have been so unobservant? How insensitive to the obvious!"

If you asked him: "How long has it been since you spent more than an hour in prevailing prayer for the lost souls of men? What is the depth of your commitment to the Lord Jesus Christ for the lost souls of men to be reached by your witnessing to them on a personal basis? What is your prayer life in relation to the millions of Muslims, Hindus, Shintoists, animists, Buddhists, Communists, atheists, humanists and nothingists who have no knowledge of God's plan of salvation or assurance of eternal life? What concern have you for the unreached millions of the world?" In all honesty he would have to answer, "Very little or none at all."

There is no fear of the Lord manifest in these sins of selfishness, prayerlessness, self-centeredness, complacency and self-righteousness. There is no acknowledgment, let alone any hatred, of these sins in the person who lives on this level.

Level Three: The sincere Christian who earnestly desires to please the Lord Jesus Christ. He does not want to sin and is deeply concerned when besetting sins are in his life. He wishes he could find an answer as to why he is always having to confess over and over again the same sins. Perhaps he commits the sins of criticism and of judging others; the sins of pride, always drawing attention to himself in conversation; the sins of unbelief in being unable to trust God, as manifest in fear, doubt and disobedience. Or maybe it is the sins of lust, covetousness, jealousy or resentment—to God or man. He is deeply concerned and longs for freedom.

Consider this rather absurd but very graphic illustration of how life is lived on this level. Just suppose there was a large deposit of cow manure on the carpet in front of a church pulpit at the start of the service. There would be one of two instinctive reactions to the cow manure. One would be to vacate the church as quickly as possible. The nearer we were to the cow manure, the more intense would be our desire to get out of the church—completely away from it. Or, our reaction would be to have someone quickly get a bucket, shovel, disinfectant and soap and get the stuff off the carpet and out of the church. Why? A very simple reason—it stinks!

Now just imagine if I were the speaker, and I said to the minister, "I need your help. I am very embarrassed that I have to tell you this. I am really going to bare my soul to you. I have a secret besetting sin. I have a secret love for cow manure! Just one whiff of it gets me. Oh, I know it is not right, and I should not be like this. I see many other people with complete victory in this area. I see that they hate it. However, I have to be honest with you; I do not hate it. It is a strong temptation to me. I have heard there is some of it on the carpet below the pulpit, and this really has me worried. I may be tempted to get into it before I even get to the pulpit. Now, I really need your prayers for me. In fact, would you pray I will be able to make it through the service, because even one whiff of it is a great temptation."

Suppose he says, "Joy, I have counseled a number of people in my life, but really, this is the most unusual thing for which I have ever been asked to pray." Then he says, "But I see you are very sincere."

If I would ask that man of God to pray for me like that, the whole thing would be as absurd as what is going on in the Body of Christ continuously. People are requesting prayer regarding their besetting sins and character weaknesses instead of coming in honesty and humility to God and saying, "I am constantly tempted to commit this sin because I love this sin. I do not hate it. I need the fear of God. O God, give me a hatred for what I now love. I receive it by faith in Jesus' name."

God will always answer that prayer. That truth is clearly shown in James 1:14–15: "But each person is tempted when he is lured and enticed by his own desire. Then desire when it has conceived gives birth to sin; and sin when it is full-grown brings forth death."

Level Four: The person who has the fear of God upon him. He hates sin; therefore, he seldom sins. If he does, there is a quick awareness of sin, immediate repentance and a willingness to humble himself before others if directed by the Holy Spirit to do so.

Proverbs 16:6 says, "By the fear of the LORD a man avoids evil." We never choose to do the thing we hate unless we know it is something that is good for us, or unless we are forced to do so by an authority over us. Right? Think it through. We have sinned because we have chosen to sin, because we love sin. The only way to be free from sin is to have God's attitude toward it, which through the fear of the Lord is to hate it. Hate sin in the mind, hate sin in word and hate sin in deed. We will hate sin in word and in deed when we hate sin in the mind because that is where it starts.

Is the deepest desire of our lives to know God, and out of that knowledge, to make Him known? If it is, then we will have to make holiness a way of life. "The friendship of the LORD is for those who fear him" (Psalm 25:14).

We can be encouraged by remembering that God created us for intimate friendship with Himself. He wants our friendship more than we want His. When in deep sincerity and faith we make one move toward Him, He makes two moves toward us. "Draw near to God and he will draw near to you" (James 4:8).

Sin not only hinders our closeness to God, but it is also destructive. Therefore we do ourselves the greatest favor by avoiding it or getting rid of it. In the next chapter we find out how we can.

6

True Repentance

If we really believe we are in the last days before the return of the Lord Jesus, we will understand the need for the preparation of the Bride of Christ to make herself ready for the "marriage supper of the Lamb."

> And I heard, as it were, the voice of a great multitude, as the sound of many waters and as the sound of mighty thunderings, saying, "Alleluia! For the Lord God Omnipotent reigns! Let us be glad and rejoice and give Him glory, for the marriage of the Lamb has come, and His wife *has made herself ready.*" And to her it was granted to be arrayed in fine linen, clean and bright, for the fine linen is the righteous acts of the saints. Then he said to me, "Write: 'Blessed are those who are called to the marriage supper of the Lamb!'" And he said to me, "These are the true sayings of God."
>
> Revelation 19:6–9, NKJV, italics added

We are hearing much about renewal, restoration, reconciliation and revival. They all hinge upon repentance because repentance among God's people precedes revival.

And every revival produces more repentance. I believe the unrepented Church (the Body of Christ) is one of the greatest hindrances to revival. "If my people who are called by my name humble themselves, and pray and seek my face, *and turn from their wicked ways*, then I will hear from heaven, and will forgive their sin and heal their land" (2 Chronicles 7:14, italics added).

God's call to bring us to repentance is an act of His love. "The goodness of God leads you to repentance" (Romans 2:4, NKJV). If we will not respond to His goodness by His forbearance and longsuffering, then He will have to come in judgment, which is another aspect of His protective love. I fully address that subject in my book *The Fire of God*. The following quotation is a small excerpt taken from it.

> God's wrath in the Bible is always judicial. That means the wrath of God administers justice. His judgment and wrath are part of His awesome holiness and absolute justice. Isaiah 5:16 says, "But the Lord of Hosts shall be exalted in judgment, and God that is holy will be sanctified in righteousness."[1]

A. W. Tozer says:

> God's wrath is His utter intolerance of whatever degrades and destroys. . . . Wherever the holiness of God confronts unholiness there is a conflict. . . . God's attitude and action in the conflict are His anger. To preserve His creation God must destroy whatever would destroy it. . . . Every wrathful

1. Joy Dawson, *The Fire of God: Discovering Its Many Life-Changing Purposes* (Shippensburg: Pa.: Destiny Image, 2005).

judgment of God in the history of the world has been a holy act of preservation. . . . He tells [us] "to flee from the wrath to come."[2]

God's judgment comes because of willful sin, and sin is the most destructive force. The suffering from judgment is meant to deter us from further sin. Judgment, therefore, is an act of God's love.

Look at what God said

to the church at Ephesus—the church who had placed other priorities before loving the Lord with all their heart: "Repent . . . or else I will come to you quickly and remove your lampstand from its place" (Revelation 2:5, NKJV).

to the compromising church at Pergamos: "Repent, or else I will come to you quickly and will fight against them with the sword of My mouth" (Revelation 2:16, NKJV).

to the corrupt church at Thyatira: "Repent or I will come with great tribulation" (see Revelation 2:22).

to the dead church at Sardis: "Repent or I'll come to you as a thief unexpectedly" (see Revelation 3:3).

to the lukewarm church at Thyatira: "As many as I love, I rebuke and chasten. Therefore be zealous and repent" (Revelation 3:19, NKJV).

Repentance has everything to do with a closer, more intimate, fulfilling relationship with the only One who can

2. A. W. Tozer, *Man: The Dwelling Place of God* (Camp Hill, Pa.: WingSpread Publishers, 1996).

meet our deepest needs. That is why the next verse says, "Behold, I stand at the door and knock. If anyone hears My voice and opens the door, I will come in to him and dine with him, and he with Me" (Revelation 3:20, NKJV). Sin dims the revelation of Jesus. "Holiness, without which no one will see the Lord" (Hebrews 12:14, NKJV). The following story vividly illustrates these truths.

I was a student at a Baptist College for four years. While there, the Lord, in answer to prayer, gave me a job to help with expenses. My work was in the Co-op store where books, supplies, candies, Cokes, coffee, and so on were sold. Occasionally, I would take a dollar or two here and there without keeping an account of it. After leaving college and the job, the Lord convicted me regarding this sin. I would worry over it, confess it to God, ask His forgiveness, *yet do nothing to settle the account.*

Listening to your taped message on knowing God would arouse deep desire to know Him better! So, I began praying repeatedly, "Lord, show me Your ways that I may know You." A few days ago God reminded me again about the matter of the sin of stealing money while employed in the Co-op. Every morning lately, I have prayed about it again. But yesterday, I truly sought the Lord as to the exact amount to send—*with interest* for the 35 or 36 years. Joy, I was shocked stiff when He revealed to me the amount. As clearly as could be, an impression came into my mind of $377! I could not believe it, but kept seeking God for confirmation. This morning just after 4:30, I was reading the booklet, *Our Daily Bread,* as follows:

Cover Up

"He that covers his sins shall not prosper" (Proverbs 28:13).

The Associated Press carried the story of an elderly man who bore the burden of a guilty conscience for 40 years. But then he decided he couldn't go on any longer without telling someone about it. So, more than 4 decades later after embezzling several thousand dollars from a bank in Washington state, he confessed his crime. When he was brought to trial, he told the judge, "After living with this thing hanging over my head for some 40 years, it got heavier and heavier until I just couldn't stand it any longer." After hearing the story, the judge showed mercy. "Criminal charges are not warranted in this case," he said, as the old man, now hard of hearing, strained to catch his words.

What a clear illustration of the fact that guilt is inescapable! Throughout the years, this man had probably tried a thousand ways to minimize, rationalize and just plain ignore that he'd done wrong. But there was no resolution until he finally admitted his crime.

Confession is the key to the problem of guilt. Over and over God urged His people to stop running from what they had done wrong and to admit their sin (Jeremiah 3:13). In the second chapter of Jeremiah, He pleads with His people, trying to get them to see where they had been unfaithful. Finally He warned them that He would judge them for denying they had done wrong, and for refusing to come back to Him for mercy (Jeremiah 2:35).

What about you today? Is there something you are covering up? It won't work. You can't elude God.

Jesus died to pay sin's debt,
Forgiveness to bestow;
But all who try to make excuse
His grace will never know.

A sin recognized is only half-corrected.
Our Daily Bread

Again God powerfully reminded me of the full quotation of Proverbs 28:13. "He who conceals his transgressions will not prosper, but he who confesses and forsakes them will obtain mercy."

I was up early today to spend time with God, but I couldn't pray. Every time I tried to pray, that big $377 was before me! God broke my heart over this sin of stealing. It was a strange time and I actually felt sick. I was quite concerned about my health, but determined to get to the bank and send the money order for $377. What a lot of money to me! But what a load is off my heart tonight for I sent the president of the college a letter of restitution with the money order.

Now I'm free from that ugly, dark pressure for the first time in many years! How I praised the Lord as I drove home, singing the hymn "Whiter Than Snow" and repeatedly praising Him for the victory through His precious blood. Now, I'm sure God will continue to "show me His ways that I may know Him"—better and better in friendship. I really want to know Him intimately. Thanks be to the Lord for your help. Now I feel that God can and will heal my back problems and answer my prayers for my non-Christian relatives. Tonight I'm so happy. I wonder if I'll be able to sleep. What a wonderful Savior He is and how He loves us to obey!

At lunch today I listened to your tape on obedience. I enjoyed it—every morsel, because my money order for stolen money plus interest had gone in the mail. Praise God!

That dear lady heard the truth, embraced the truth, acted upon the truth and has been set free by the One who is the Truth. She is on her way to experiencing friendship with God at completely new levels. No wonder she is happy!

Notice the first part of Hebrews 12:14. "Pursue peace with all people" (NKJV). So often our repentance is needed in our relationships with others. We are only as close to the Lord as we are close to the person we love the least. "If someone says, 'I love God,' and hates his brother, he is a liar; for he who does not love his brother whom he has seen, how can he love God whom he has not seen? And this commandment we have from Him: that he who loves God must love his brother also" (1 John 4:20–21, NKJV).

Repentance is the way out—the way of escape—when we have failed to live by the biblical standards. It means having a change of mind, heart and life toward sin. We need to understand the priority of this message in Jesus' ministry when He was on earth and its priority in the early Church.

Jesus' first message was "Repent." "From that time Jesus began to preach and to say, 'Repent, for the kingdom of heaven is at hand'" (Matthew 4:17, NKJV). Jesus' subsequent teaching after John the Baptist was arrested was the same. "The time is fulfilled, and the kingdom of God is at hand. Repent, and believe in the gospel" (Mark 1:15, NKJV). He taught His twelve disciples to teach the same. "They went out and preached that people should repent" (Mark 6:12, NKJV).

Luke alone records another ten references to repentance in the preaching of the Lord Jesus.

In the last discourse of Jesus with His disciples, He said plainly that the whole purpose of His death and resurrection was that "repentance and remission of sins should be preached in His name to all nations" (Luke 24:47, NKJV).

Repentance was at the heart of Peter's message on the Day of Pentecost (see Acts 2:38). Paul preached, "Now [God] commands all men everywhere to repent, because He has appointed a day on which He will judge the world in righteousness by the Man whom He has ordained" (Acts 17:30–31). We need to understand that there is repentance of sin in the general sense for salvation, and then repentance of specific sins following conversion. There is no such thing as general confession of sin. For example, "If I have sinned, forgive me." God always convicts us of specific sins.

There is no other way to get rid of specific sins than to repent of them. "Repent therefore and be converted, that your sins may be blotted out, so that times of refreshing may come from the presence of the Lord" (Acts 3:19, NKJV). In Job 36:8–12 we read:

> If they are bound in fetters, held in the cords of affliction, then He tells them their work and their transgressions—that they have acted defiantly. He also opens their ear to instruction, and commands that they turn from iniquity. If they obey and serve Him, they shall spend their days in prosperity, and their years in pleasures. But if they do not obey, they shall perish by the sword, and they shall die without knowledge.
>
> NKJV

Also in Proverbs 29:1 we read: "He who is often rebuked, and hardens his neck, *will suddenly be destroyed, and that without remedy*" (NKJV, italics added).

Satan tempts us by telling us the lie, "Sin and no one will know." God says, "Be sure your sin will find you out" (Numbers 32:23, NKJV).

Satan says, "Sin and you will get away with it." God says, "Whatever a man sows, that he will also reap" (Galatians 6:7, NKJV).

For example, a farmer in a Midwestern state in the United States who was opposed to Christianity was overtly hostile to Christians as they went to church on Sunday morning while he plowed his fields. In October the farmer had the best crop of anyone in his entire county. He put a belittling advertisement in the paper related to Christians and finished it with, "Faith in God must not mean much if someone like me can prosper." The Christians responded in the next edition with, "God doesn't always settle His accounts in October."

While God is amazingly patient and longsuffering, we must realize that He does not let us get away with anything. Sin always has its consequences. There comes a time when God moves in on us and lets us know that He does not bend His rules for anyone. He is not Father Christmas. In Hebrews 10:30–31 we read, " 'The Lord will judge His people.' It is a fearful thing to fall into the hands of the living God."

Remorse is our reaction to how our sin has affected ourselves.

Regret is our reaction to how our sin has affected others.

Repentance is how we respond to sin from God's perspective from His Word and how it has affected God and others.

7

How Do We Repent?

We must first realize the necessity of conviction of sin, by the Holy Spirit. It may come when we are not asking for it. Our conscience may be stirred. It may come when we are reading God's Word, or when we are listening to teaching or preaching from the Bible. We may not want conviction, but conviction of sin is a wonderful gift from God. It is "doctor" God warning us that there is a spiritual disease in us producing destruction to our spirits, minds, souls and bodies. We have a choice to listen to a medical doctor's diagnosis, ask for the cure and apply the treatment. So we have a choice in relation to conviction of sin. If we want to be whole and to have a closer relationship with God, we will submit to "doctor" God.

We can also invite God to give us the gift and blessing of conviction of sin by praying the following prayers:

> Search me, O God, and know my heart; try me, and know my anxieties [thoughts]; and see if there is any wicked way in me, and lead me in the way everlasting.
>
> Psalm 139:23–24, NKJV

How many are my iniquities and my sins? Make me know my transgression and my sin.

Job 13:23, NKJV

Who can understand his errors? Cleanse me from secret faults.

Psalm 19:12, NKJV

Wait in God's presence and give Him time to answer. Humility of heart does this as a way of life. Pride avoids it.

The first step following conviction is to agree with God that we have not lived up to His standard in His Word. "Therefore, to him who knows to do good and does not do it, to him it is sin" (James 4:17, NKJV). Then confess it with our lips. "If we confess our sins, He is faithful and just to forgive us our sins and to cleanse us from all unrighteousness" (1 John 1:9, NKJV). We now *change our mind* toward that sin. "I am choosing to go God's way, not mine in relation to it."

There is a vast difference between confession of sin and repentance. In Proverbs 28:13–14 we read, "He who conceals his transgressions will not prosper, but he who confesses and *forsakes them* will obtain mercy. Blessed is the man who fears the LORD always; but he who hardens his heart will fall into calamity." Second Timothy 2:19 says, "Nevertheless the solid foundation of God stands, having this seal: 'The Lord knows those who are His', and, 'Let everyone who names the name of Christ *depart from iniquity*'" (NKJV, italics mine).

Pharaoh is an example of someone who confessed sin but never repented. "Then Pharaoh sent, and called Moses and Aaron, and said to them, 'I have sinned this time; the LORD is in the right, and I and my people are in the wrong'" (Exodus 9:27). Moses' reply is very significant. In verse 30 we read, "But as for you and your servants, I know that you do not yet fear the LORD God." The lack of Pharaoh's repentance was evidenced by his subsequent actions in verse 34, "But when Pharaoh saw that the rain and the hail and the thunder had ceased, he sinned yet again, and hardened his heart, he and his servants."

Saul is another example of confession without repentance. After David had asked Saul why he was trying to kill him, Saul actually wept as he realized how wrong he was, but he never repented of the sin. "He said to David, 'You are more righteous than I; for you have repaid me good, whereas I have repaid you evil'" (1 Samuel 24:17). He then committed the same sin again and when challenged by David he said, "I have done wrong; return, my son David, for I will no more do you harm, because my life was precious in your eyes this day; behold, I have played the fool, and have erred exceedingly" (1 Samuel 26:21). He confessed the fruit of sin—attempted murder—but never dealt with the roots of jealousy and pride.

We are now ready for a *change of heart*. We acknowledge the reason we chose to sin was because we wanted to. There was a desire for that sin in our hearts. We read in Proverbs 8:13, "The fear of the LORD is hatred of evil." We obviously need a change of desire in our hearts from loving sin to hating it. We ask for the fear of the Lord in relation to that sin and receive it by faith. We are asking God for His attitude toward sin. "By the fear of the LORD a man avoids evil" (Proverbs 16:6).

Proverbs 28:14 says, "Blessed is the man who fears the LORD always [hates sin and wants to get rid of it]; but he who hardens his heart will fall into calamity." When we fear God we want to repent of sin.

Next we need to see the sin from God's perspective. We need to find out what the Bible says about our particular sin. This means searching the Scriptures. As we do, we need to pray, "Lord, show me not only what You think about this sin, but how You feel about it." Then we need to pray, "Show me my heart as You see it." We read in 2 Chronicles 6:30–31: "Give to everyone according to all his ways, *whose heart You know* (for You alone know the hearts of the sons of men), that they may fear You, to walk in Your ways as long as they live" (NKJV, italics mine). Also we need to ask God to reveal to us the motives behind our actions. "There are those who are pure in their own eyes but are not cleansed of their filth" (Proverbs 30:12).

God may answer those prayers immediately. He did that once with me. It resulted in the revelation of my heart that caused me to bring mild correction to others, while being blind to my own failures. It was a life-changing experience, as I wept before God and those to whom I had sinned against, naming the root sin of pride.

It may also mean wrestling with God like Jacob did, before the revelation comes. God uses this method to test us to see how much we really want this spiritual heart surgery. It is devastating to see our hearts as God sees them—the root sins of pride or unbelief. At the same time it is wonderful, because it is so liberating. Jesus said, "You will know the truth, and the truth will make you free" (John 8:32). In my book *The Fire of God*, I have written in detail the accounts of the times God has answered my prayers for a revelation of my heart, and the ensuing results. And in my Resource Guide, there is an audiotape available from my message, "The Release of the Spirit through Brokenness." This message has been uniquely used by God to bring liberation to many. The main point is to pray until the revelation comes.

I have an international Bible teacher friend who heard me speak on this subject many times during a seven-year period. She would seek God after each hearing, but never wait in His presence long enough for Him to release the revelation of her heart. Finally, she told God she would stay alone in His presence until it came, no matter what the cost. She told me that after seven protracted hours of waiting on God, He met her at a deep level. He revealed that the root sin of pride affected almost every area of her life. It was horrible—but absolutely life-changing.

This dear woman of God released me to use her experience whenever the Holy Spirit prompted me. She wanted it to be a severe warning to others not to resist the Holy Spirit by not applying the truths when we hear them. Of course, I have chosen to withhold her name. At the same time, I am so grateful for her willingness to share.

Our knowledge of truth brings our accountability to God to obey it. In His justice, God has to weigh up His judgments with us in the light of those who would gladly obey Him if they had the opportunity to hear the truth.

8

Other Influences
That Affect Our Choices

We may need to ask God to show us if there are other areas in our lives that have influenced us to sin. For example, we may need to be set free from a hereditary bondage. My precious husband has asked me to share his story to illustrate this point.

I had been puzzled over many years of marriage as to why Jim would use humor to say little belittling things about me in front of others. But he never did this when we were alone with each other. One day I gently approached the subject, reminding him that I had observed that his father did exactly the same thing in relation to his mother. Jim's parents had a lifetime close relationship and had long since gone to heaven.

Jim had been previously unaware of the effect of these behavior patterns, but acknowledged that what I had shared was valid. He repented before God and asked for my forgiveness, which was freely given. We realized that this was a hereditary bondage, so we took our authority in the name of the Lord Jesus Christ over these influences. We bound them according to Matthew 18:18 and commanded their power over Jim to be broken. We praised God for the power in God's Word and in Jesus' name and shed blood to set Jim free. He was completely liberated. "So if the Son makes you free, you will be free indeed" (John 8:36).

Some years later, we were on a ministry trip to Scotland and went to visit a cousin of Jim's who was the vicar of a church. Jim's parents were originally from Scotland before emigrating to New Zealand, where Jim was born. Sitting around a dining room table, we happened to mention to Jim's cousin the changes that had taken place in Jim and in our marriage, from what I have just shared. His cousin immediately explained that the behavior patterns in Jim's father came from his being brought up in Fife Shire. It was a way of life in that area to belittle people in humor—an inbuilt characteristic. He also confirmed the absolute need to have broken that hereditary bondage in the way that we did.

As an international missionary family who loves humor, we were strong offenders with ethnic jokes until the Holy Spirit deeply convicted us. Thank God for His mercy. All ethnic jokes are inconsistent with the biblical standard of humility and love, because they are always belittling. We must never use humor when it is at the expense of demeaning others. Pride is the cause.

The Word of God links together humility and love. Here are some examples: "With all lowliness and meekness, with patience, forbearing one another in love, eager to maintain the unity of the Spirit in the bond of peace" (Ephesians 4:2–3). "Love one another with brotherly affection; outdo one another in showing honor" (Romans 12:10).

We can also be acting or reacting negatively because of a traumatic experience from the past, from which we need healing. Our human spirit may have been wounded. The Holy Spirit will reveal if this is the cause and will release His power to heal those painful memories.

We come in simple faith and ask the Father in Jesus' powerful name to do just that, provided we have fully forgiven those who have hurt us. I have seen wonderful results, many times, of the supernatural healing of the subconscious mind. Believe God's promise in Isaiah 53:4–5: "Surely he has borne our griefs and carried our sorrows; yet we esteemed him stricken, smitten by God, and afflicted. . . . Upon him was the chastisement that made us whole, and with his stripes we are healed." I am aware that it is often very difficult to forgive those who have hurt us. But God assures us that His enabling power is available to us. "See to it that no one fail to obtain the grace of God; that no 'root of bitterness' spring up and cause trouble, and by it the many become defiled" (Hebrews 12:15).

When the following principles are applied and maintained, total forgiveness is assured:

1. We must realize that forgiveness is an act of the will. We have to want to forgive. Actually, we do ourselves a favor because resentment is a strongly destructive

force to our minds, our bodies, our souls and our spirits. "A tranquil mind gives life to the flesh, but passion makes the bones rot" (Proverbs 14:30).

2. Realize you will not be forgiven by God unless you forgive others who have hurt you. "If you forgive men their trespasses, your heavenly Father also will forgive you; but if you do not forgive men their trespasses, neither will your Father forgive your trespasses" (Matthew 6:14–15). "And whenever you stand praying, forgive, if you have anything against any one; so that your Father also who is in heaven may forgive you your trespasses" (Mark 11:25).

3. Think of all that God has forgiven you. "Be kind to one another, tenderhearted, forgiving one another, as God in Christ forgave you" (Ephesians 4:32). "As the Lord has forgiven you, so you also must forgive" (Colossians 3:13).

4. Thank the Lord for any or all of the blessings He has brought to you through the person who has hurt you. "Give thanks in all circumstances; for this is the will of God in Christ Jesus for you" (1 Thessalonians 5:18).

5. Think of the needs of the person at the time of hurting you—needs of their mind, body, soul and spirit. Their needs, then and now, are probably greater than yours.

6. Ask God to give you His supernatural ability to love them and forgive them through you and receive this by faith. This becomes a miracle, because without the oncoming of the Holy Spirit, we will not come to freedom. "God's love has been poured into our hearts through

the Holy Spirit which has been given to us" (Romans 5:5). "Without faith it is impossible to please him. For whoever would draw near to God must believe that he exists and that he rewards those who seek him" (Hebrews 11:6).

7. Ask God to give you opportunities of expressing His love to them both in word and in deed. "But if any one has the world's goods and sees his brother in need, yet closes his heart against him, how does God's love abide in him? Little children, let us not love in word or speech but in deed and in truth" (1 John 3:17–18).

8. Become an intercessor for them. Pray for God to bless them, encourage them, comfort them, strengthen them and meet their deepest needs. "But I say to you, Love your enemies and pray for those who persecute you" (Matthew 5:44).

9. When we have fully forgiven others, we will not want to speak about how they have wronged us. "And above all things have fervent love for one another, for 'love will cover a multitude of sins'" (1 Peter 4:8, NKJV).

Panic attacks can occur irrationally, coming from frightening experiences of the past. Ask God to bring them to your remembrance and pray for those memories to be healed. Release faith in God's promises to deliver you, that are in His Word. "For God has not given us a spirit of fear, but of power and of love and of a sound mind" (2 Timothy 1:7, NKJV). "I sought the LORD, and he answered me, and delivered me from all my fears" (Psalm 34:4).

Now we are ready for a *change of life*. We have determined that these sins will no longer be a part of us, so we ask God to show us how to change our habit patterns, believing that He will.

The keys are always found in God's Word. "If you continue in my word, you are truly my disciples, and you will know the truth, and the truth will make you free" (John 8:31–32). It is very helpful to search the Scriptures for what they have to say about habitual sins. For example, if you are having trouble controlling your tongue (who doesn't?), make a list of the Bible verses that address that subject and meditate on them often. That method works wonders!

Repentance includes humbling ourselves and making restitution to anyone we have wronged as God directs us. Paul addresses this in Acts 26:20: "They should repent and turn to God and perform deeds worthy of their repentance." I believe that we should be prepared to humble ourselves before at least one person, as well as God, naming our sin and asking for that one to pray for us. The power of the Spirit is uniquely released upon us when we humble ourselves before those whom God will give us for that purpose. Isaiah 66:2: "But this is the man to whom I will look, he that is humble and contrite in spirit, and trembles at my word." God knows who can be trusted with our broken and contrite spirit. "Therefore confess your sins to one another, and pray for one another, that you may be healed" (James 5:16).

We are now ready to ask God to have mercy on us, and not give us what we deserve. The prophet Habakkuk understood this when he prayed, "in wrath remember mercy" (Habakkuk 3:2). David understood it deeply, too. Listen to his cry. "Be merciful to me, O Lord, for I cry to You all day long. . . . For You, Lord, are good, and ready to forgive, and abundant in mercy to all those who call upon You" (Psalm 86:3–5, NKJV).

Thank God that His mercy is always extended to a truly repentant heart, and to the level we are prepared to humble ourselves before others. When we declare our sin to another, we can have the added benefit of asking that person to stand in the gap before God on our behalf, asking Him to extend more mercy to us. I have watched these principles work powerfully over my lifetime and in the lives of others.

We not only receive by faith God's forgiveness and mercy, but we forgive ourselves because God has. This is often a struggle. It has been with me. What has helped me is to realize that I am insulting God's mercy and ability to forgive and forget my sins, as well as limiting the power of His shed blood to cleanse me, if I keep dragging them up to myself. Micah 7:18–19 is so comforting to a truly repentant heart.

Who is a God like You, pardoning iniquity and passing over the transgression of the remnant of His heritage? He does not retain His anger forever, because He delights in mercy. He will again have compassion on us, and will subdue our iniquities. You will cast all our sins into the depths of the sea.

NKJV

Finally, it is important that we declare in faith that, in daily submission to the enabling power of the Holy Spirit's control, we will remain free. "Stand fast therefore in the liberty by which Christ has made us free, and do not be entangled again with a yoke of bondage" (Galatians 5:1, NKJV).

A healthy spiritual exercise is to frequently check the following list to see if there is need for repentance in our lives:

- all phonyism and inconsistency,
- prayerlessness, impurity of motive,
- lack of witnessing, lack of unity,
- jealousy, resentment, competitiveness,
- judging, criticism, the fear of men,
- rebellion, unbelief, the love of money,
- materialism, disobedience,
- all sexual impurity,
- disobedience to the Great Commission,
- a disregard for the sanctity of marriage,
- no fear of God—no real hatred of sin,
- insufficient time with God in His Word studying His character and ways,
- pride—robbing God of His glory by self-promotion and seeking the recognition of men,
- unbelief—in God's ability to powerfully work through us,
- presumption—through the lack of waiting on God and seeking His face for direction—until He speaks, and

- allowing the spirit of the world to influence our thinking and behavior.

Purposes for Repentance of Sin

1. To stop grieving the Lord Jesus, who paid the horrendous price to deliver us from the ravages of sin by His death on the cross (see 2 Corinthians 5:21).
2. To prevent quenching the Holy Spirit's power to enable us for God's service (see 1 Thessalonians 5:19).
3. To enable us to fulfill our destinies by becoming more like Jesus (see Romans 8:29).
4. To enable us to be in intimate friendship with Him and find fulfillment (see Psalm 25:14).
5. To keep us from the most destructive force to our minds, bodies, souls and spirits. "The wages of sin is death" (Romans 6:23).
6. To enable us to share our faith more effectively and bring more people to Jesus (see Matthew 4:19; Proverbs 11:30; Acts 1:8).
7. To stop holding back the revival and spiritual awakening we desperately need; to turn from our wicked ways of pride, unbelief and prayerlessness (see 2 Chronicles 7:14).
8. To prepare us to be part of His spotless Bride for the marriage supper of the Lamb (see Ephesians 5:27; Revelation 19:6–7).
9. To prepare us for standing at the judgment seat of Christ, where we will give an account of what we did

with the opportunities He gave us to know Him and make Him known (see 2 Corinthians 5:10).

10. To prepare us for serving Him throughout eternity. How we live here on earth determines what sort of privileges and responsibilities we will be given in heaven.

9

Our Thought Lives

All sin starts in the mind; therefore, we are only as holy as our "thought lives" are holy. "For as he thinketh in his heart, so is he" (Proverbs 23:7, KJV).

I believe our thoughts sound as loudly in heaven as our words do on earth. "The thoughts of the wicked are an abomination to the LORD, the words of the pure are pleasing to him" (Proverbs 15:26). Would we want our thoughts to be written on a wall at the end of a day for anyone to see? God has done it before; He can do it again!

In Daniel 5:24–28, we read how God sovereignly wrote on the wall of King Belshazzar's palace His assessment of the king's life and the judgment resulting from it. That night the king died.

When the woman was caught in the act of adultery and brought by her accusers to Jesus, twice we read in John 8 that Jesus "bent down and wrote with his finger on the ground" (verses 6, 8). By the time Jesus had finished writing, there was no one left of the woman's accusers, showing that in either thought or deed, all were guilty of the same sin.

It is not sufficient to repent of sin committed with our words and actions alone. Repentance of our sinful thoughts is equally important. "Let the wicked forsake his way, and the unrighteous man *his thoughts*; let him return to the LORD, that he may have mercy on him, and to our God, for he will abundantly pardon" (Isaiah 55:7, italics added). "Let the words of my mouth and the *meditation of my heart* be acceptable in thy sight, O LORD, my rock and my redeemer" (Psalm 19:14, italics added).

When David was repenting of the sin of adultery, as recorded in Psalm 51:6, he said to God, "Behold, thou desirest truth in the inward being; therefore teach me wisdom in my secret heart." The *inward being* and the *secret heart* refer to his thought life. He knew what every person knows who has committed acts of immorality, that the act with the body starts with the sin of lust in the mind. That is why David asked for wisdom in his secret heart, which means the fear of the Lord upon his thought life, because "the fear of the LORD is the beginning of wisdom" (Psalm 111:10).

In His Sermon on the Mount Jesus confirmed this principle and tied it into the seventh commandment: "Every one who looks at a woman lustfully has already committed adultery with her in his heart" (Matthew 5:28).

God explains why He is totally unimpressed with a man's service and sacrifice when he is unfaithful to his wife:

And this again you do. You cover the LORD's altar with tears, with weeping and groaning because he no longer regards the offering or accepts it with favor at your hand. You ask, "Why does he not?" Because the LORD was witness to the covenant between you and the wife of your youth, to whom you have been faithless, though she is your companion and your wife by covenant. Has not the one God made and sustained for us the spirit of life? And what does he desire? Godly offspring. So take heed to yourselves, and let none be faithless.

Malachi 2:13–15

Satan can come at any point in time and tempt us with any kind of sin. It does not matter what it is: unbelief, lust, pride, criticism, disobedience to God or anything. We will find there is no attraction to that temptation to sin to the degree that we have been asking for the fear of God and receiving it by faith. We will have Jesus' attitude toward sin, and instantly we will say to Satan, "Nothing doing! I happen to hate your suggestion and I am not about to do what I hate. I resist you in the name of the Lord Jesus Christ. It is written in James 4:7, 'Resist the devil and he will flee from you.'"

God tells us to replace that evil thought with pure ones. "Whatever is true, whatever is honorable, whatever is just, whatever is pure, whatever is lovely, whatever is gracious, if there is any excellence, if there is anything worthy of praise, think about these things" (Philippians 4:8). The Amplified Bible says, "Fix your minds on them." That is a deliberate, determined, disciplined act of your will.

Think of the face of the Lord Jesus Christ. Look at a beautiful flower or scenery, and worship the Creator. Quote or read the Word of God aloud. Sing praises to God. Sing hymns or Scripture verses. Light is stronger than darkness. Keep turning on the light! Truth is stronger than error. Keep declaring it! "Do not be overcome by evil, but overcome evil with good" (Romans 12:21).

How do we know when evil thoughts come into our minds if they are satanic in origin or from our own hearts? The answer is very simple—by our immediate reaction to these thoughts. If we have an immediate reaction of hatred to them, we know they never came from our hearts. The thoughts came, therefore, from satanic activity upon our minds. If we have not had an immediate reaction of hatred to some critical, evil, unforgiving, lustful or unbelieving thought, then we know there is still a love for that sin in our hearts. We know we have homework to do in that area. We need to ask for the fear of the Lord to come upon us to replace the love for that sin.

If we are bombarded continually in any one area of our Christian life with satanic attacks, we will know demonic spirits have been listening to what is coming out of our mouths or they have been observing what we are doing. Evil spirits are not omniscient. They do not have all knowledge. They cannot read our thoughts. Satan is a destroyer and will always attack us where we are weak and vulnerable. He knows our weaknesses by hearing the things we are saying and by seeing the things we are doing. "For out of the abundance of the heart [or mind] the mouth speaks" (Matthew 12:34). So our greatest need is for the fear of God to be upon our thought lives, where all sin starts.

The prophet Ezekiel was given revelation into the thought lives of spiritual leaders. The first thing he saw was the jealousy in their hearts. Then he saw their idolatry. Ezekiel 8:12 says, "Son of man, have you seen what the elders of the house of Israel are doing in the dark, every man in his room of pictures? For they say, 'The Lord does not see us, the Lord has forsaken the land.'"

We are only as pure as our thought lives are pure. All our ministries are only as powerful as our thought lives are clean. Where we have men, women, young people and children who have chosen to have the fear of the Lord upon them, who are asking God for it frequently and who are receiving it by faith, we have purity of minds and a basis for the Holy Spirit to release His power in the Church.

The following is the story of a young woman who wrote to me after hearing one of my taped messages on the fear of the Lord.

I realize now that I have never feared the Lord as He intends. Until just today, I've been fighting a really tough battle with my thought life; and although I *know* to "make no provision for the flesh," as Paul says in Romans 13:14, and to do all the things I know are necessary to combat these temptations, still they have persisted.

The temptation and the sin that followed was immorality in my thought life. I have been a Christian for six years, but my husband is not.

At night, I would dream about another young man to whom I was attracted, although there had never been an immoral word or action pass between us. But I *knew*, and I knew that he *knew* that something sensual was there. Words are hardly necessary. Eyes do it. Right? I would cry out to God for help, but really felt that He wasn't hearing me because as Psalm 66:18 says, "If I regard iniquity in my heart, the Lord will not hear me" (KJV).

She went on to say that she found an answer to her problem through my telling of an incident that happened while I was teaching at a Youth With A Mission's School of Evangelism in Switzerland. I told the students they needed to prepare their hearts before the Lord before partaking of Communion, as we are exhorted to do in 1 Corinthians 11:27–29:

> Whoever, therefore, eats the bread or drinks the cup of the Lord in an unworthy manner will be guilty of profaning the body and blood of the Lord. Let a man examine himself, and so eat of the bread and drink of the cup. For any one who eats and drinks without discerning the body eats and drinks judgment upon himself.

Time was given for the students to seek God diligently, asking Him to reveal anything in their lives that needed to be put right. If and when they knew they had the peace of God that accompanies a clean heart, they were to feel free to participate.

One young woman came to me privately and shared that she had no release from the Holy Spirit to partake of Communion but had no idea why. She asked me to seek God on her behalf. I did.

What followed was very enlightening! God revealed to me by His Spirit that she lacked the fear of God in her relationships with the opposite sex. This was being evidenced through her personality, and by the way she dressed; both were being used to arouse sexual desire in young men. I shared this with her.

There was an immediate witness in her spirit that this was truth, and she quickly acknowledged it. She deeply repented before God, and asked Him to give her a hatred of this sin, which is based in pride.

She told God she would go to several of the male students whom she was particularly aware of having tempted and ask their forgiveness at the first opportunity. Then she partook of the elements with a clean heart.

Her testimony over the ensuing years has been that it was a life-changing experience. I know her well, and the fear of God marks her life.

The woman who had listened to this story continued to tell me in her letter that she strongly identified with it. As a result, she knew she was going to have to follow the same principles of repentance and seeking God's forgiveness.

She wrote, "The Lord has used this whole thing to teach me that if we name our sin for what it is, repent of it, ask for and receive His forgiveness, cry out for the fear of God, and make restitution if and as He directs us, then He is faithful and just to forgive us. My obedience to these truths diffused the lust!"

I believe a strong word of caution is needed here. We need to be very careful in relation to making restitution to others. We need to seek God with diligence for His wisdom to be given us,

1. if we are to communicate to others at all,
2. to whom we are to communicate,
3. when to communicate and
4. how to communicate.

He has promised in Psalm 32:8–9, "I will instruct you and teach you the way you should go; I will counsel you with my eye upon you. Be not like a horse or a mule, without understanding, which must be curbed with bit and bridle, else it will not keep with you."

I know of a young married man who went to a single girl and confessed he was having lustful thoughts toward her, and asked her forgiveness. Yet he did this without the fear of God upon him in relation to his lust. He still loved it.

Previously she was totally unaware of this. But *after this communication*, she found herself sinning toward him in her mind in exactly the same way. She, too, had no fear of God in relation to this sin.

It was not long before they both committed adultery physically.

Psalm 111:10 says, "The fear of the LORD is the beginning of wisdom; a good understanding have all those who practice it." If he had truly repented of the sin of lust, cried out to God for a hatred of it and received that by faith, he would have had the wisdom, in this case, to know *not* to communicate his sin to the one to whom it was directed.

After the inevitable mess and sorrow that follows adultery, I am delighted to add that both parties genuinely saw their desperate need for the fear of the Lord, repented, made full restitution and were completely restored to full fellowship with God. Both went on to living vital Christian lives—separately from one another.

The following chapter spells out how our relationship with God is only as holy as our relationships with each other, and that the fear of God makes both relationships exciting.

10

Relationships: Holy or Unholy

The fear of the Lord is the answer to all problems connected with relationships—whether with the opposite sex or with the same sex.

In order for us to understand what God intends us to experience in relationships here on earth, we first have to look at the model He has given us. We find it in John 17, where Jesus prays to the Father for the ultimate: "That they [all believers] may be one, even as we [the Trinity] are one" (verse 11). That means that within the limitations of our humanity, we can experience through the power of the Holy Spirit the same quality of love that exists among the Father, Son and Holy Spirit.

I will never forget when that amazing truth hit me, and I really believed it for the first time. A number of years ago, I was in a room in Denmark, praying with three married couples—all missionaries. God had broken through by His Spirit and brought real brokenness and openness among them. I was experiencing such an outpouring of the love of God toward them that I asked the Holy Spirit to give me the greatest possible prayer I could pray for each couple. Then I waited in expectancy for the answer.

It did not come quickly. God was testing me as to how long I would wait to get the maximum request. I remember responding while I continued to wait: *I love them, Lord. They are worth waiting for.* After some time, the Holy Spirit brought to my mind with great clarity Jesus' prayer: "That they may be one, even as we are one."

As I prayed in faith for the greatest blessing-prayer that could be released from headquarters heaven for human relationships on planet earth, there was an explosion of revelation and excitement in my spirit that day that has never left me. For I then realized this was God's norm for all our relationships as Christians—regardless of whether the combination includes old or young, single or married, male or female. After all, the quality of love emanating from the Godhead is the same to everyone, and I believe it is expressed in the same way. So why should it be any different when it flows through us to anyone else?

I cannot imagine Jesus expressing His love any differently to Mary and Martha than to Lazarus. Nor can I think for a moment He would experience any awkwardness in any area of His relationships with them—collectively or separately. Not even when He was alone with lovely, marriageable, deeply spiritual, devoted Mary as she sat at His feet, listening to His teaching. I do not expect she was looking out the window either. She would be looking into His eyes, drinking in every word, as she did on another occasion when Jesus was in Bethany with His disciples: "Mary took a pound of costly ointment of pure nard and anointed the feet of Jesus and wiped his feet with her hair; and the house was filled with the fragrance of the ointment" (John 12:3).

The scenes are intimate, without any sexual connotation! There is no embarrassment or sin, because there is no guilt—in either party.

Let us switch scenes.

Jesus is now in the house of a Pharisee having a meal, and an ex-prostitute hears He is there. (See Luke 7:36–50.) She seizes the opportunity of getting close to Him, away from the inevitable crowds that always followed Him.

She gate-crashes the party and immediately proceeds to open up her alabaster flask of ointment. Then she demonstratively bursts into tears, which splash over His feet. Undaunted by the cold, critical stares of the Pharisee host, she uses her long hair to mop up the tear stains, and unashamedly kisses Jesus' feet and then anoints them with the ointment.

She lavishly expresses the devotion and gratitude of her heart to the only One who has ever shown her such love, such forgiveness, such mercy, such recognition, such respect, and who has given her such peace of mind. Does all this display of affection faze Jesus? Is He embarrassed? No! He is totally relaxed. With calm authority, He rebukes the religious host and praises the repentant woman from the streets. Again the scene is intimate, without sexual connotation.

None of this should really surprise us when we understand that one of the purposes of Jesus Christ's leaving heaven and coming to this earth was to show us how to live. For that reason, we can see He was demonstrating through the relationships with those two women that true holiness and naturalness go hand in hand.

In fact, only really holy people are free to be really natural.

They have nothing to hide.

There is no need to act.

There is nothing to cover up.

With the fear of the Lord upon us, we are able to experience the kind of love that Peter talks about in 1 Peter 1:22 (NIV) and express it to anyone at any time. "Now that you have purified yourselves by obeying the truth so that you have sincere love for your brothers, love one another deeply, from the heart."

Throughout God's Word, we find love and holiness are frequently linked together. Holiness in thought, word and deed releases us to be loving and tender in our relationships without a particle of lust. In 1 Thessalonians 3:12–13, we read, "And may the Lord make you increase and abound in love to one another and to all men, as we do to you, so that he may establish your hearts unblamable in holiness before our God and Father, at the coming of our Lord Jesus with all his saints." Also, in Philippians 1:9–10, we find, "And it is my prayer that your love may abound more and more, with knowledge and all discernment, so that you may approve what is excellent, and may be pure and blameless for the day of Christ."

These verses make it clear that we are not to be afraid of the depth of love toward one another, provided every relationship can stand the test of the bright, white light of the Holy Spirit's standard of purity in thought, word and deed.

God the Father entrusted His Son with the close friendships of women such as Mary of Bethany and Mary Magdalene, as well as Peter, James and John. Hebrews 4:15 says, "[He] was in all points tempted like as we are, yet without sin" (KJV). According to this verse, He had to suffer temptation, which would include the area of friendships, in order to become our understanding High Priest and Intercessor.

My understanding of human relationships deepened when I saw that only God can totally fulfill any human being; therefore, no human being will ever totally fulfill me—or you. When God leads a man and a woman together in a marriage relationship, provided they live together according to His ways, those two people will complement each other, meet needs in each other and be to each other in numerous ways what no one else will ever be. In other words, it is a unique relationship of a type that can be experienced only by the total joining together and commitment of marriage.

However, marriage was never intended by God to be an all-inclusive thing in regard to human relationships; otherwise, there would be no justice to the single person. There would also be no room for a Jesus and Mary relationship (both Mary of Bethany and Mary Magdalene), or a Jesus and John, or a David and Jonathan. These were all very close relationships outside marriage.

God delights to give in-depth friendships to His children, in proportion to the fear of God operating in their lives, regardless of their sex. So, we cannot expect every area of our lives, even in relation to friendship fulfillment, to be found in marriage alone.

Now, let us look more closely at God the Father, God the Son and God the Holy Spirit. The more we understand the nature of this relationship and the principles by which they operate, the more we can cooperate with the Lord Jesus in the fulfillment of His prayer for Trinity unity (John 17:11) among His present disciples.

Let us measure our relationships—any and all of them— alongside God's standard for us, which is the relationship of the Trinity:

1. God the Father, Christ the Son and the Holy Spirit are equal in authority but different in function.
2. They complete each other in ministry function—never compete. Often we are unaware where one starts and another ends; there is a total blending of the three.
3. They are totally dependent on each other, based on the humility that knows they desperately need each other.
4. They have absolute truth in their relationships, therefore, absolute trust.
5. They glorify one another and serve one another.
6. They have singleness of purpose.
7. They have absolute holiness in all their relationships, and therefore they experience the ultimate in enjoyment of one another.

8. They are an invincible team, who have an eternal indestructible Kingdom, and who achieve the ultimate in effectiveness.

Look again at number seven: "They have absolute holiness in all their relationships." When we really believe this truth, we come to understand that any relationship is only pleasurable, purposeful and fulfilling to the degree that the fear of God remains the basis of the relationship.

The devil has convinced millions of people of the lie that a little or a lot of sin makes any relationship more exciting. Nothing is further from the truth. Sin eventually produces deadness; holiness brings abundant life.

Jesus said, "The thief comes only to steal and kill and destroy; I came that they may have life, and have it abundantly" (John 10:10).

The devil says, "Sin. You'll get away with it."

God says, "Do not be deceived; God is not mocked, for whatever a man sows, that he will also reap. For he who sows to his own flesh will from the flesh reap corruption; but he who sows to the Spirit will from the Spirit reap eternal life" (Galatians 6:7–8). "Some were sick through their sinful ways, and because of their iniquities suffered affliction" (Psalm 107:17).

The devil says, "Sin. No one will know."

God says, "Be sure your sin will find you out" (Numbers 32:23). "Therefore do not pronounce judgment before the time, before the Lord comes, who will bring to light the things now hidden in darkness and will disclose the purposes of the heart" (1 Corinthians 4:5).

115

God says, "Nothing is covered up that will not be revealed, or hidden that will not be known. Therefore whatever you have said in the dark shall be heard in the light, and what you have whispered in private rooms shall be proclaimed upon the housetops" (Luke 12:2–3).

The Bible says Satan is a tempter, a murderer, a liar, a deceiver, a thief, the father of lies and a destroyer. How he deceives us in the area of sex is discussed in the next chapter.

11

God's Gift of Sex

Satan is loudly and distinctly proclaiming his viewpoint about sex through both open and subtle means of communication—from pornography in literature and in movies, to commercial advertisements. He says, "I can make sex more exciting. I know far more about it than anyone else. Listen to what I have to say. Look at what I have to offer. I'll really enlighten you. Then you'll experience the ultimate enjoyment."

It is high time that lie was exposed. The truth is, Satan does not happen to be the author or creator of this wonderful gift. God is. Therefore, God knows infinitely more about it than anyone else.

Only in obedience to His laws, obeying the rules He has laid down in His Word, will we ever be able to fulfill all He intended through this gift. It was given for procreation, comfort and enjoyment, as well as a means of helping to maintain the romantic love God gave us for one another.

Satan's second lie about sex (aimed mostly at Christians) is that it is dirty, and anyone who wants to be truly holy will have nothing to do with it. The reason I know this is because Christian women have communicated this to me on a number of occasions. God answers that in James 1:16–17 by saying, "Do not be deceived, my beloved brethren. Every good endowment and every perfect gift is from above, coming down from the Father of lights with whom there is no variation or shadow due to change." Also in 1 Corinthians 7:5, Paul exhorts married couples who are not living together naturally in the physical realm, "Do not refuse one another except perhaps by agreement for a season, that you may devote yourselves to prayer; but then come together again, lest Satan tempt you through lack of self-control."

When I was about nine years old, one of my brothers, who was ten-and-a-half years old, told me he had asked my father (an outstanding Christian, evangelist and Bible teacher) how it was that he could be like my father, and yet have come from inside my mother.

My father had answered my brother in the natural, direct way in which he communicated everything, telling him the facts about conception. My brother, in turn, related them to me in exactly the same way.

A little later, while on my own, walking down a path toward the beach, I was pondering this new thing I had learned about how life was formed. I was filled with awe, and wonder, and worship, and love to God. I marveled at His power, His knowledge and His wisdom that He had worked out a plan as Creator in making two bodies that would fit together when they needed to, in order to keep the human race propagated. I gave Him the pure worship that was due to Him. God, sex, naturalness, purity and worship have always been correlated in my thinking. God has done everything to make those factors correlate in the human race. Satan has done everything to distort and separate them. The purest mind in the universe thought up the whole fantastic idea of sexual relations between men and women. The purer our minds are, the more we will worship God for this wonderful gift.

God created men and women with a desire for sexual expression, and He has given clear guidelines for that fulfillment within marriage—and only within marriage. In His infinite knowledge, wisdom, justice and love, He knows what is best for us spiritually, mentally, emotionally and physically. Humility bows to that, and obeys. Pride rebels and disobeys.

Satan says to us exactly what he said to Eve: "Don't take God literally. Don't take Him that seriously."

Satan says to us today, "In this enlightened, modern age, that just does not apply. Our culture is different. Everybody indulges sexually. It is an appetite that needs feeding. You'll be frustrated and repressed if you don't."

God says, "The body is not meant for immorality, but for the Lord, and the Lord for the body. And God raised the Lord and will also raise us up by his power. Do you not know that your bodies are members of Christ? Shall I therefore take the members of Christ and make them members of a prostitute? Never! Do you not know that he who joins himself to a prostitute becomes one body with her? For, as it is written, 'The two shall become one flesh.' But he who is united to the Lord becomes one spirit with him. Shun immorality. Every other sin which a man commits is outside the body; but the immoral man sins against his own body. Do you not know that your body is a temple of the Holy Spirit within you, which you have from God? You are not your own; you were bought with a price. So glorify God in your body" (1 Corinthians 6:13–20).

God says, "You shall not commit adultery" (Exodus 20:14).

God says, "Do you not know that the unrighteous will not inherit the kingdom of God? Do not be deceived; neither the immoral, nor idolaters, nor adulterers, nor sexual perverts, nor thieves, nor the greedy, nor drunkards, nor revilers, nor robbers will inherit the kingdom of God" (1 Corinthians 6:9–10).

God says, "But as for the cowardly, the faithless, the polluted, as for murderers, fornicators, sorcerers, idolaters, and all liars, their lot shall be in the lake that burns with fire and sulphur, which is the second death" (Revelation 21:8).

It is spelled out quite clearly, isn't it? We either obey Satan's lies and choose death, or we obey God's truth and choose eternal life.

Homosexuality and lesbianism are included in immorality. God says, "You shall not lie with a male as with a woman; it is an abomination" (Leviticus 18:22).

God says, "If a man lies with a male as with a woman, both of them have committed an abomination; they shall be put to death, their blood is upon them" (Leviticus 20:13).

God says, "But nothing unclean shall enter it [the New Jerusalem], nor any one who practices abomination or falsehood, but only those who are written in the Lamb's book of life" (Revelation 21:27).

God is looking for men and women whom He can trust. So He tests us in many ways to see whether we can be taken into closer friendship with Himself, and to see whether we can be given greater responsibilities and privileges in His Kingdom.

One of the ways He tests us is to put us closely in service for Him alongside members of the opposite sex. We can be attracted to them in four major ways: by spiritual unity, by mental affinity, by personality compatibility and by physical attraction. We can be conscious of any one, or all four of these attractions in a relationship.

By far the deepest attraction is spiritual unity. Without the fear of the Lord, it is the easiest thing in the world to fall for the temptations of Satan—first of all in the thought life, then in word and deed. Multiplied thousands do; they succumb to immorality, bringing dishonor to the name of the Lord Jesus Christ and great sorrow to themselves and others.

The non-Christian looks on and says, "What is the difference between the Christian and me? He does the same things!" So the professing Christian without the fear of the Lord becomes the worst advertisement to Christianity, and God has another big disappointment on His hands.

But then, to God's great delight, He finds men and women in the Body of Christ who have chosen to walk the highway of holiness (Isaiah 35:8), who have chosen the fear of the Lord as Jesus did, who have said, "We delight in holiness," who have made a study of holiness from the Word of God, who have made it a passion and priority of life, who constantly ask for it and receive it by faith, and who frequently go into His school via Psalm 34. They would rather be in a move of God's Spirit where His holiness is manifest than any other move of His Spirit on earth.

When God finds such people, He says, "All right. Now, I can trust you. I can take you and team you with people who have any one or all of those four attractions. I can take you and team you with any man, any woman, in any situation. . . . I can trust you."

When He trusts us, we never want to fail Him!

What trust! What privilege! Is it hard? Is it difficult? No, it is not difficult. It is easy. Do you know why it is easy? Because when we hate sin, we want no part of it.

When God finds a man or a woman who hates sin as He hates it, and will obey Him, do you know what God has? A man or a woman with whom He can do anything. Anything! Holiness and obedience go hand in hand. Obedience is the manifestation of holiness and love for Jesus. "The end of the matter; all has been heard. Fear God, and keep his commandments; for this is the whole duty of man" (Ecclesiastes 12:13).

God will now put His authority on us, and He will give us the privileges and responsibilities in His Kingdom that He will not give to those who do not have it. "He who fears God shall come forth from them all" (Ecclesiastes 7:18).

One day I received a letter from a woman who had been reading a copy of the first edition of this book. She expressed deep gratitude. Her story is as follows. She and her husband were Christians and they had several children. Although she had a genuine hunger for a deeper understanding of God's character and ways, to her disappointment, her husband did not evidence that same desire. But she prayed and longed for that fulfillment.

When she came to the teaching in this chapter, she was aware of how much she needed to heed God's warnings. She read about the four attractions we all have toward the opposite sex: physical attraction, personality compatibility, mental affinity and spiritual unity. She read that by far the deepest attraction is spiritual unity. I went on to explain that God can test us to see how much He can trust us, by putting us alongside others in team ministry with any or all four of those attractions. In times of satanic temptation, without the fear of the Lord, which is to hate evil, we will fail the test. But with the fear of the Lord we will live in victory and overcome the temptation.

She pondered these truths deeply. The more she did, she realized that God had already tested her by allowing her to be teamed with the opposite sex as they related to the first three attractions, and she had passed the tests. But she had never been tested by being in close teamwork with a man with whom she had a deep spiritual unity.

She realized the profound truth of her utter vulnerability, because of the lack of her relationship with her husband in this area. She shared with me that she kept weeping before the

Lord in sheer gratitude that in His love and faithfulness to her, He had brought her to this book and these truths to forewarn her. She said, "To be forewarned is to be forearmed."

I was deeply touched by the depth of understanding this dear woman had that *only* the fear of the Lord will cause us not to fall for the subtlety of the enemy's devices. She knew she needed to be crying out for more of the fear of the Lord as a way of life. Of the many encouraging letters I gratefully receive, this one was especially so. I trust the woman's starkly honest testimony will be used of God to speak to others.

In the next chapter, we take a look at the choice every woman makes in her relationships with men.

12

The Power of a Woman's Influence

Women have great ability to influence others—for good or evil. Wouldn't that be the reason the serpent approached Eve in the Garden of Eden?

When God made woman for man, He said her role was to be a "helper fit for him" (Genesis 2:18). Through her influence, a woman either helps a man to be holy or hinders a man from being holy. A woman is either a stepping-stone, which makes the pathway easier, or she is a stumbling block, which makes it more difficult in relation to holiness.

Because of the power of a woman's influence for evil, it is significant that there are three passages in Proverbs warning men about immoral women (Proverbs 2:16–19; Proverbs 5; and Proverbs 6:20–35).

Note the admonition in Proverbs 6:23–29:

For the commandment is a lamp and the teaching a light, and the reproofs of discipline are the way of life, to preserve you from the evil woman, from the smooth tongue of the adventuress. Do not desire her beauty in your heart, and do not let her capture you with her eyelashes; for a harlot may be hired for a loaf of bread, but an adulteress stalks a man's very life. Can a man carry fire in his bosom and his clothes not be burned? Or can one walk upon hot coals and his feet not be scorched? So is he who goes in to his neighbor's wife; none who touches her will go unpunished.

The adulterer is further rebuked in Proverbs 6:32–33: "He who commits adultery has no sense; he who does it destroys himself. Wounds and dishonor will he get, and his disgrace will not be wiped away."

There is also a special warning to leaders to guard against immoral women in Proverbs 31:3: "Give not your strength to women, your ways to those who destroy kings."

The king who had the greatest heritage, honor, riches, wisdom, opportunity and potential was Solomon. Yet, we read this tragic account of him in 1 Kings 11:4: "For when Solomon was old his wives turned away his heart after other gods." The influence of foreign women was the strongest source of temptation for him to choose sin. God knew they would be; that is why He told Solomon not to marry them.

The failure of women to exert a godly influence can produce devastating results:

What if Eve had chosen to obey God, when Satan tempted both Adam and her to sin, by exerting her God-given influence on Adam? It is far less likely Adam would have chosen to disobey God, regardless of his failure to protect Eve from Satan's devices. Remember, the Bible says that "Adam was not deceived" (1 Timothy 2:14).

What if Bathsheba had said a polite, firm "No, thank you" when David suggested committing adultery? I do not believe David would have ever raped her! What tragedy would have been averted.

What if she had said, "David, think of the implications that would inevitably come from this sin. We would both be sinning against God and our marriage partners. And greater accountability, and therefore judgment from God, would be upon you because of your level of leadership. We both know very well the commandment, 'Thou shalt not commit adultery.' And besides, Uriah is such an honorable husband it would be utter folly to betray his trust in me." (It is evident from the account of Uriah's reactions to David's suggestions that Uriah was a man of principle and integrity. See 2 Samuel 11:9–11.)

What if Sarah had encouraged Abraham to tell the full truth about her being his wife and had urged him to trust God with their lives when they went into a new city? I do not think Abraham would have lied on two occasions by saying she was his sister.

What if she had said, "Now Abraham, because of the culture in this part of the world, I can understand your fear that the men of this city may kill you in order to have sexual relations with me. But we need to stop and think about the character of God. He did not give me this kind of physical beauty in order for us to live in fear of my being raped or your being killed. Lies are never justified or consistent with the fear of God. Let us commit ourselves into God's all-powerful hand and pray down the fear of God upon these men as we tell the truth. I believe we will have a story of God's miraculous intervention, and I can hardly wait to see it happen!"

There is another wonderful side to this coin of truth. God has devoted nearly the entire chapter of Proverbs 31 to the description of a virtuous woman. It is very significant that the first mark of her virtue is "the heart of her husband trusts in her" (Proverbs 31:11). I am convinced that the secret to that trust is found at the end of the chapter in verse 30: "Charm is deceitful, and beauty is vain, but *a woman who fears the LORD is to be praised*" (italics added). That means a husband can be assured of his wife's faithfulness only to the degree he knows she fears God, and vice versa.

The influence of a holy woman cannot be measured. Many times I have heard the testimonies of men (many of them great men) who have shared that the greatest influence toward holiness in their lives has come from women.

The Bible gives us some powerful examples of godly women who exerted their influence toward men. The results speak for themselves.

One day an angel appeared to Manoah's wife while she was out in the field and told her she was going to have a son. She had been barren for many years. As incredible as that sounded to her, she heard the angel continue to say that the child would begin to deliver Israel from the hand of the Philistines! No small announcement, right out of the blue!

This woman of humility and faith simply and totally believed the heavenly messenger and promptly reported the facts to her husband, Manoah. The strength of conviction with which she spoke would have greatly influenced him to believe God for the impossible in the natural—which he certainly did. Samson was the result of their faith. (See Judges 13.)

If ever a woman had a difficult role to play, it was Abigail. Through her humility, wisdom and swift action at the time of great crisis, she powerfully influenced David, the future king, against making major mistakes as a leader. At the same time, she saved the lives of her household and staff. (See 1 Samuel 25.)

Queen Esther went against the king's decree and laid her life on the line by appearing in the king's court, even though she was not summoned by him. She used her influence with the king to plead for the lives of her people, the Jews, as they were facing annihilation as a nation. Her request was granted. (See Esther 7.)

An in-depth, personal encounter with the Lord Jesus at lunchtime, by a well, produced a startling difference in a notorious woman. So powerful was the testimony of her changed life, that the whole city of Sychar in Samaria was influenced by it. (See John 4.)

As a wife and a mother of great faith, Jochebed powerfully influenced her three children who all became spiritual leaders—Moses, Aaron and Miriam (see Micah 6:4). They, in turn, became people of great faith. What a unique family.

The strength of Hannah's godly influence on her little boy, Samuel, was immeasurable. His life was marked by the fear of the Lord—so much so that in 1 Samuel 12:18 we read that the people feared the Lord *and* Samuel. As a result, the course of history in Israel at that time was radically changed toward righteousness.

In Judges 4 we find Deborah, the prophetess and judge, strongly motivating the general Barak to go into battle against the Lord's enemies. Because of her leadership and teamwork with other leaders, a mighty victory resulted from the battle. Special mention is made of the key role she played in the victory song: "The peasantry ceased in Israel, they ceased until you arose, Deborah, arose as a mother in Israel" (Judges 5:7).

All of these women were history makers.

Each woman today needs to understand and accept the strength of her God-given influence, choose to be the greatest possible influence toward holiness to every male who comes across the pathway of her life and pray fervently it will be so. The fear of the Lord makes it so. She then needs to exercise that influence in obedience to the promptings of the Holy Spirit. What responsibility! What accountability! What privilege! What opportunity!

We are discovering there are many aspects to the fear of the Lord. The next one I had to learn about in a very humbling way as God dealt heavily with me. I am deeply grateful to Him that He did because it greatly helped to change my life, as you shall see in the next chapter.

13

Touching the Lord's Anointed

God makes it clear from a number of Scriptures that we are not to criticize and judge others. "Judge not, that you be not judged. For with the judgment you pronounce you will be judged, and the measure you give will be the measure you get" (Matthew 7:1–2). "Do not speak evil against one another, brethren. . . . Who are you that you judge your neighbor?" (James 4:11–12).

The Word of God makes it equally clear that there is an added dimension of God's judgment when the criticism is against those in positions of spiritual authority. We need to understand the weight of God's command in Psalm 105:15: "Touch not my anointed ones, do my prophets no harm!"

When Miriam, the prophetess and leader, criticized her leader-brother Moses, God's judgment came upon her in the form of leprosy (see Numbers 12:9–10).

Korah, Abiram and Dathan came under God's heavy judgment when they spoke against and led other leaders into criticism and rebellion against Moses and Aaron. God opened up the ground around them and they went down to their death as the earth closed over them (see Numbers 16).

Michal, who was Saul's daughter and David's wife, had a barren womb for the rest of her life because she spoke against the Lord's anointed, David. She despised him in her heart, and she spoke critically to him about the way in which he expressed praise to the Lord in a time of victory.

Forty-two youths who jeered at the prophet Elisha when he was walking along the road were mauled by bears (2 Kings 2:23–24).

On the other hand, David gives us a classic example of what it means to obey the injunction of "not touching the Lord's anointed." Even though Saul was pursuing David with the intent of murder, he was still the leader of Israel. God had not yet removed him from that office. David respected that, and because of the fear of the Lord upon him, he would do nothing to harm Saul.

The principles learned from these lives apply to us today.

It is very significant that the live coal off the altar for the preacher Isaiah was for purging his lips. (See Isaiah 6.)

God can use a preacher's tongue only to the degree the preacher has allowed God to tame it and control it.

There is a very pertinent message for those who preach and teach in Jeremiah 15:19: "If you utter what is precious, and not what is worthless, you shall be as my mouth." Or, as another version says, "If thou take forth the precious from the vile, thou shalt be as my mouth" (KJV). I have lived to see some of the strongest judgments of God on people who have touched the Lord's anointed. So often these situations have been in the area of one spiritual leader wrongly judging another. One of the quickest ways to grieve the Holy Spirit and have barrenness of soul is to speak against another person who is in spiritual authority.

We do not have to agree with everything other preachers or spiritual leaders say, but we should not speak against them in a way that would deter people from receiving the *good* from their ministry.

Let us accentuate the positive when reporting on other ministries. Let us encourage people to grow and be under the influence of what we know is of God and is good in them. Then, if we are still concerned, commit them to the Lord in prayer and say, "Lord, there are things I do not agree with or understand, and if my concern for them is valid, I trust You to work in them and to lead them into what You know is truth." Just because we do not understand something they have said or done does not mean we have all knowledge or have a right to judge. It is possible that something may be strange to us because we have not gone deep enough with God to understand it. It is equally possible they are in error.

Even when we know a spiritual leader, or anyone else, is wrong in some matter, we must guard against letting that wrong get out of proportion in our thinking to all the things in him that are right. If we think or talk about the life and ministry of a person only as it relates to areas that need correction, we get that person out of perspective to the way God sees him.

God accentuates the positive, not the negative, in His thoughts toward us. That is why He is so merciful, long-suffering and kind, although He never overlooks our sin.

I will never ever forget, many years ago, when God burned this truth on the fleshy table of my heart, and it has permanently remained with me. I was attending a convention where I was placed in charge of counseling for women. There was a deep move of God's Spirit in the fear of the Lord.

I had been counseling a woman under the direction of the Holy Spirit, and her needs were obviously being met. Suddenly, all knowledge of what I was to do next left me. We both knew God had not completed His purposes in our being together.

When I asked God to show me if there was some blockage in me that would cause His Spirit to cease flowing through me in the release of His wisdom and knowledge, I came under conviction of sin. God reminded me that earlier in the day I had made a casual derogatory remark to my husband about one of the speakers at the convention. It was in connection with a brief conversation I had had with the speaker earlier in the day. I also remembered confessing my sin a little later to God in front of my husband, *but I had not seen that sin as God sees it*; therefore, my confession and repentance were shallow.

I had "touched the Lord's anointed," and God wanted to impress upon me the gravity of that sin in His sight. As the conviction became deeper, I fell to my knees and cried out to God for mercy. Then the conviction increased until I was lying on the floor groaning under the weight of it. This time repentance was very deep. When I finally felt God's peace restored to me, I got up and went back to being available to God on behalf of the woman. Immediately, clear impressions came to my mind related to meeting the woman's needs. God was again releasing His wisdom through me.

A change took place in my life that day—a very humbling and very necessary one. I understood in a new and deeper way the truth of Hebrews 12:10: God "disciplines us for our good, that we may share his holiness."

This point is so important, I believe God would have me give another illustration. I know of a speaker who had weekend meetings in a large church. There was a young woman in that church who was totally unknown to the preacher. On the Sunday night following the service, she had gone home and then to bed. In the middle of the night she was awakened with severe pain in her head and spine, although she had gone to bed in perfect health.

That night, the preacher had spoken on what to do when things go wrong. The first point was to ask God the question, "What is it You are trying to teach me?" A number of possible answers were then taught from the Word of God.

One of them was that undealt-with sin in our lives can be the cause of the adverse circumstances. She remembered this point.

So, she cried out to God and asked, "Is there some undealt-with sin in my life that I should awaken with this violent pain?"

The Holy Spirit said, *Yes, you have criticized the preacher who spoke tonight.*

"Oh, God, yes," she responded. The Holy Spirit reminded her how she had criticized the speaker to her husband as well as to others in the church service that night. She confessed this before the Lord and repented of her sin. Immediately, the pain lifted from her back.

In the morning the pain was still in her head, so she asked God if there was anything else she needed to do.

He said, *There needs to be restitution. You need to humble yourself.*

She telephoned the church office and said, "I need to speak to the visiting preacher." They replied, "It is not our policy to disturb our visiting speakers after a tiring weekend of ministry, but the pastor's wife is in the office if you would like to speak to her."

As she started to unburden her heart to the pastor's wife and to humble herself before her, she said, "God has reminded me that I did exactly the same thing when this preacher came to our church a year ago." (At that time, she was a brand-new Christian, and God had permitted her to get away with it as a new babe in Christ. However, a year later, it was a different story.) She said, "Never before had I understood God's view on this sin, but I do now. When I confessed this sin last night, immediately the pain left my spine. I know no more to do than to tell you everything and to ask you to tell all of this to the preacher."

As she humbled herself in obedience to God, He then released the pain in her head. The law of humbling is very important in the law of confession and restitution. James 5:16 says, "Therefore confess your sins to one another, and pray for one another, that you may be healed."

That young woman was set free. God received her humbling and her repentance.

If we are in a position of spiritual authority and have to deal with someone in error within our sphere of authority, the Bible gives us a clear plan of action:

> Brethren, if a man is overtaken in any trespass, you who are spiritual should restore him in a spirit of gentleness. Look to yourself, lest you too be tempted.
>
> Galatians 6:1

> If your brother sins against you, go and tell him his fault, between you and him alone. If he listens to you, you have gained your brother. But if he does not listen, take one or two others along with you, that every word may be confirmed by the evidence of two or three witnesses. If he refuses to listen to them, tell it to the church; and if he refuses to listen even to the church, let him be to you as a Gentile and a tax collector.
>
> Matthew 18:15–17

> Never admit any charge against an elder except on the evidence of two or three witnesses.
>
> 1 Timothy 5:19

> This is the third time I am coming to you. Any charge must be sustained by the evidence of two or three witnesses.
>
> 2 Corinthians 13:1

Approaching the right people at the right time to carry out these injunctions is important. As we seek God, He will reveal both. Ecclesiastes 8:5 says, "He who obeys a command will meet no harm, and the mind of a wise man will know the time and way."

When correction and discipline need to be given to a truly repentant, humble person, it is important that it is carried out according to God's character. God's love and mercy must be balanced with His holiness, judgment and justice:

> I believe the most balanced view of God's character that is summed up in one verse of the Bible is found in Jeremiah 9:24: "let him who glories, glory in this that he understands and knows Me, That I am the Lord, exercising loving kindness, judgment and righteousness in the earth. For in these I delight, says the Lord."

Loving kindness	**Judgment**	**Righteousness**
(long-suffering and merciful)	(justice)	(holiness)

So, God delights equally in displaying Himself in these three main attributes from which all His other attributes flow. When we major on any one of them more than another, we obviously have an unbalanced view of Him, which inevitably produces constant confusion or incorrect descriptions and explanations of Him. From God's viewpoint, the subject of Himself as a God of Judgment is all too seldom spoken about today, and as a result many people are ignorant. "But My people do not know the judgment of the Lord." Jeremiah 8:7.

In Jeremiah 5, God goes to great lengths to explain His justice when operating in Judgment. I love the way God links the subject of His judgment with pursuing truth, when He tells His people to look everywhere and see if we can find anyone who "executes judgment, who seeks truth." Jeremiah 5:1.

If we really want to know the truth about who God is, we must study and embrace His judgment equally along with His other attributes. It also means that when we have to exercise judgment we must be zealous to have all the facts before we do.

Then in Jeremiah 5, verses 4 and 5, God goes further and makes some startling statements about spiritual maturity and the lack of it: (1) people who don't understand the judgment of God are both foolish and don't know the way of the Lord. (2) Truly great men know both. Think about that. "Therefore I said, Surely these are poor; they are foolish; for they don't know the way of the Lord, the judgment of their God. I will go to the great men and speak to them, for they have known the way of the Lord, the judgment of their God."

I also believe we will never understand God or His ways without studying His justice. It has been one of the most rewarding Biblical pursuits of my life. It has been pivotal to my search for the knowledge of God, in order to effectively make Him known.[3]

A repentant person who has been given a disciplinary edict has every right to question anything that he or she considers not consistent with the character of God. That is a part of God's justice. In my Resource Guide I have two

3. Dawson, *The Fire of God*, 127. Used by permission.

audiotaped messages titled, "The Justice of God in Leadership." A VHS videotaped message is also available titled "Understanding God's Justice." If we are dealing with someone under our leadership who is in error, we need to make sure we are fulfilling all the heart preparations that follow.

When we sincerely believe a spiritual leader over us is wrong, we should act in the fear of God toward that person as follows:

1. Make absolutely sure we have all the facts correct and we are not reaching conclusions from hearsay or presumption. John 7:24 says, "Do not judge by appearances, but judge with right judgment." We need to constantly remind ourselves that only God knows the up-to-date situation of every human heart. We may be wrongly judging someone because repentance has taken place without our knowledge of it.

2. Invite the Holy Spirit to search our hearts and to reveal any resentment or critical attitude toward that leader, and repent if there is conviction. Hebrews 12:14–15 states, "Strive for peace with all men, and for the holiness without which no one will see the Lord. See to it that no one fail to obtain the grace of God; that no 'root of bitterness' spring up and cause trouble, and by it the many become defiled."

3. Ask God to touch our hearts with His love toward that leader, and thank Him that He will. "Above all hold unfailing your love for one another, since love covers a multitude of sins" (1 Peter 4:8).

4. Recognize it is the work of the Holy Spirit to release that love in us, and submit to His control. "The love of God is shed abroad in our hearts by the Holy Ghost" (Romans 5:5, KJV).

5. Thank God for the blessings we have received through that leader, and acknowledge the blessings that have come through him to others. "With thanksgiving let your requests be made known to God" (Philippians 4:6).

6. Pray that God will meet his deepest need, reveal to him what is truth and motivate him to walk in it. Continue to pray this in faith. Do not make suggestions to God what the need of that leader may be.

7. We should not share our concern with another unless prompted to do so by the Holy Spirit and unless we know the person's heart has been deeply prepared like our own. Then, together intercede for the leader in the same way.

8. If over a period of time, there is no sign of change in the leader, pray that God will reveal the need to other people who have the spiritual authority to deal with the problem. Also, pray they will deal with it according to biblical principles.

9. Commit the leader into God's hands, and ask Him to do something that will bring the maximum glory to His name in the situation, and believe He will.

If the leader walks "in the light, as he is in the light" (1 John 1:7), God will vindicate that person in time, regardless of past mistakes or of his innocence.

"Therefore do not pronounce judgment before the time, before the Lord comes, who will bring to light the things now hidden in darkness and will disclose the purposes of the heart. Then every man will receive his commendation from God" (1 Corinthians 4:5).

"No weapon that is fashioned against you shall prosper, and you shall confute every tongue that rises against you in judgment. This is the heritage of the servants of the LORD and their vindication from me, says the LORD" (Isaiah 54:17).

If the leader does not walk in the light, then God will fulfill His Word: "The sins of some men are conspicuous, pointing to judgment, but the sins of others appear later" (1 Timothy 5:24). "For nothing is hid that shall not be made manifest, nor anything secret that shall not be known and come to light" (Luke 8:17).

14

Encouragement

We may be realizing just how little of the fear of God we have operating in our lives. Praise God, His mercy is always extended to a truly repentant heart. Joshua 3:5 is a wonderfully encouraging truth: "Sanctify yourselves; for tomorrow the LORD will do wonders among you."

I am glad He is the God of tomorrow's fresh plans, despite today's mistakes.

> Who is a God like thee, pardoning iniquity and passing over transgression for the remnant of his inheritance? He does not retain his anger for ever because he delights in steadfast love. He will *again* have compassion upon us, he will tread our iniquities under foot. Thou wilt cast all our sins into the depths of the sea.
>
> Micah 7:18–19, italics added

When we truly humble ourselves before God and man, where God requires that of us, and when we start walking the highway of holiness spoken of in Isaiah 35:8, our areas of greatest weakness can become our areas of greatest strength. That is good news!

Remember, Moses was a murderer, and he later became a man of whom God said, "And there has not arisen a prophet since in Israel like Moses, whom the LORD knew face to face" (Deuteronomy 34:10).

David was a murderer and an adulterer, who later gave us the classic prayer of repentance in Psalm 51, who reached tremendous heights of praise and worship and who became a man after God's own heart who would do all God's will as described in Acts 13:22.

Job was self-righteous and resentful toward God during the latter part of his testing; but after a fresh revelation of God he said, "I despise myself, and repent in dust and ashes" (Job 42:6). God's response was, "And the LORD restored the fortunes of Job, when he had prayed for his friends; and the LORD gave Job twice as much as he had before" (Job 42:10).

King Nebuchadnezzar was proud, and he refused to acknowledge the supreme authority and sovereignty of God. He came under God's heavy judgment: "He was driven from among men, and ate grass like an ox" (Daniel 4:33). After repentance and full restoration, he not only gave one of the most magnificent testimonies in the Bible about the justice of God, but God added still more greatness to him (verses 36–37).

We never need to be in despair that we will not attain to intimate friendship with God. Being obedient to the next thing God tells us to do will get us there. That is not complicated.

He has promised to clearly communicate to us everything we will ever need to know in order to obey Him, provided we want to obey. "I will instruct you and teach you the way you should go; I will counsel you with my eye upon you" (Psalm 32:8).

We can also be encouraged to know that God always rewards diligent seekers. "And without faith it is impossible to please him. For whoever would draw near to God must believe that he exists and that he rewards those who seek him" (Hebrews 11:6).

With the simplicity of a child, we can come to our loving heavenly Father and trust Him to lead us one step at a time along the pathway of obedience that leads to intimate friendship with Him. He is longing to take our hand and do just that.

Like a child who is learning to walk, if we fall, He will be there to pick us up and help us take the next step . . . and the next, until obedience to Him becomes a way of life.

Check in the final section of this book under "Essentials for Progress as a Christian." That is a good place to start.

15

Idolatry and the Fear of the Lord

It is possible to think we have the fear of the Lord operating in our lives when we have none, or very little, according to God's standards. In 2 Kings 17 we find a classic example of this.

The people concerned came under the judgment of God, because "they did not fear the LORD" (verse 25). Next, verse 26 states that they did not know what the Word of God said. Usually these two conditions go together.

Then the king of Assyria commanded that a priest be sent to live among them and to teach them these priorities.

The subsequent verses tell us they wanted to have their cake and eat it, too. They chose to continue in idolatry, yet expected to have benefits from God by being involved with religious pursuits. This made them phonies, and it did not work. Verse 33 says, "So they feared the LORD but also served their own gods."

But God makes it very clear in the next verse that their fear of God was merely terminology. He says, "They do not fear the LORD, and they do not follow the statutes or the ordinances or the law or the commandment which the LORD commanded the children of Jacob, whom he named Israel."

We have the fear of the Lord upon us only to the degree we say and believe that the Word of God is our standard of righteousness, and to the level we match up to this in every area of our daily living.

In this chapter God makes it very clear that from His perspective we have the fear of God upon us only in proportion to our freedom from idolatry. An idol is something or someone that takes a priority place in our lives over the Lord Jesus Christ in our thinking, in our time, in our affection, in our loyalty and in our obedience.

It is significant that the *first* commandment is, "You shall have no other gods before *me*" (Exodus 20:3, italics added). We know we are living in obedience to that commandment when we can say with joyful, enthusiastic conviction, "All my springs are in you" (Psalm 87:7).

In the Bible, God makes it clear that idolatry is a symptom of "heart trouble." This malady can, and often does, exist in the midst of regular church attendance and involvement in much Christian activity.

The prophet Ezekiel received a message from God of strong rebuke to give to some of the elders of Israel when they came to inquire of him as to the word of the Lord. God told Ezekiel that because of the idolatry in the hearts of those elders, He would not give the prophet *anything* to say to them, but that He would speak to them directly through bringing judgment upon them! (See Ezekiel 14:1–8.) In these verses, God is concerned about the heart being distant, cold and estranged toward Him because other things had taken His place. In verse 5, He says, "That I may lay hold of the hearts of the house of Israel, who are all estranged from me through their idols."

The heavier our spiritual responsibilities become by virtue of our level of leadership and/or ministry function, the more easily we can allow the ministry itself to become the center of our focus and the pivot of our priorities—idolatry! We need to ask ourselves:

What thrills us the most?

What do we think about the most?

What do we talk about the most?

What gets our time and attention the most?

Possessions? Money? Investments? Food? Sexual gratification? Job promotion? Authority? Travel? Home? Hobbies? Higher education? Sports? Television? Leaders? Spiritual leaders? Friends? Family? Project achievements? Fulfillment of vision? Ministry? Leisure time? The pursuit of pleasure?

In Hosea 14:8–9, we are given a graphic description of the insanity of idolatry as God calls out to Ephraim with a yearning, loving, parent heart. Let us put our name in the place of Ephraim's as we read the following verse: "O Ephraim, what have I to do with idols? It is I who answer and look after you. I am like an evergreen cypress, from me comes your fruit."

I believe God is saying here, "I am the One who gave you mortal life and eternal life, answered your prayers, looked after you when no one else was there, protected you, comforted you, directed you, understood you, loved you with an everlasting love, gave you strength and power, motivated you to make the right choices, energized you by My Spirit and used you to help others. Nothing else nor anyone else has done this for you. I am the source of your life. Why put the pursuit of other things before the pursuit of knowing Me in order to make Me known? *None of these idols can fulfill you!*"

Perhaps now we can better understand the importance of the Lord Jesus' own words in Matthew 22:37: "You shall love the Lord your God with all your heart, and with all your soul, and with all your mind." It is the only thing that makes any sense in the light of who He is and what He has done.

In Jeremiah 2:11, God speaks about the absolute futility of idolatry: "Has a nation changed its gods, even though they are no gods? But my people have changed their glory for that which does not profit."

When God stops to think about His people substituting *anything* for Himself, the all-sufficient I AM, as their supreme love and purpose for living, He breaks out into strong language of utter amazement and says in the next verse:

"Be *appalled*, O heavens, at this, be *shocked*, be *utterly desolate*, says the LORD, for my people [not the unbelievers] have committed two evils: they have forsaken me, the fountain of living waters, and hewed out cisterns for themselves, broken cisterns, that can hold no water" (italics added).

Did you notice that God's intense reaction was not because they had forsaken *serving* Him—but because they had forsaken *Him*?

Have you ever pondered the loneliness of God? He created us for friendship with Himself, yet we give Him relatively little time for intimacy!

We may consider ourselves to be mature Christians because we spend much time in Bible study, intercession for others and seeking Him frequently for wisdom and guidance; yet we give Him little time for a love relationship.

We may also think that more time or money spent on pleasing ourselves would bring us greater happiness. If we do, we try to protect ourselves from being too involved or too committed in service to God and others.

Or, even if we are heavily involved in ministering to others with little time for ourselves, we can often be thinking in our hearts, *The nearest thing to heaven would be to go fishing, or to play golf, or read a book* (or other forms of relaxation).

The truth is, the more we are available to God on behalf of others without considering ourselves, in time, the more He will plan surprises and treats for us that will include doing the things we enjoy the most. And it is always in a way that is far beyond anything we could plan.

Our God is absolutely just, and He is a magnificent master. For every right I have ever relinquished to Him and for every step of obedience I have taken to His directions, He has abundantly rewarded me and blessed me and my family beyond anything I have deserved or could have imagined.

I firmly believe "the nearest thing to heaven" is being in the center of the will of God, delighting to do His will and delighting myself in Him, my lover God, who planned that part of His will for me, regardless of where on this globe that may be.

That is freedom. That is fulfillment. The privileges and rewards from God when we truly place Him first in undivided devotion far outweigh the price—no matter how high.

In 2 Kings 23 and in Deuteronomy 9, when the people of God were truly turning away from their idolatry, their leaders broke the idols, ground them to powder, burned them to dust and ashes and threw away the dust! That is true repentance.

If we will not repent of the things in our lives that take a priority place over the Lord Himself, He will bring His judgment upon us in those very areas.

Idolatry usually takes place gradually and subtly; therefore, we are often blind to it until the Holy Spirit reveals it to us.

A dear woman of God, who is a Bible teacher, told me that a fire broke out one day in her sewing room. As she inquired of the Lord as to why this had happened, He revealed to her that she had been putting her hobby of sewing before her pursuit of God. She had been disobedient to God's priorities for her life. Her repentance released God's forgiveness and mercy to her, as well as greater wisdom.

A minister friend once told me something that made an indelible impression upon me. He said one day God used a bottle of ink that spilled all across the pages of his open Bible while he was studying, to reveal idolatry to him. The

Holy Spirit convicted him of having a greater love for Bible study than for God Himself.

When we name our idols before God (and man if God prompts us to), and repent of them by a change of mind, heart and life, God does His part to deliver us and to set us free. He is our deliverer.

"I will sprinkle clean water upon you, and you shall be clean from all your uncleannesses, and from all your idols I will cleanse you" (Ezekiel 36:25).

"And I will deliver you from all your uncleannesses; and I will summon the grain and make it abundant and lay no famine upon you" (Ezekiel 36:29, italics added).

16

What It Takes to Obtain the Fear of the Lord

We are told, "The fear of the LORD is the beginning of wisdom; a good understanding have all those who practice it" (Psalm 111:10). Then we read, "The fear of the LORD is the beginning of knowledge" (Proverbs 1:7). Also, "The fear of the LORD is instruction in wisdom" (Proverbs 15:33).

If the fear of the Lord is the beginning of knowledge and the beginning of wisdom, then the fear of the Lord is the beginning. *Have we begun?*

The question is not, "What is our ministry in the Body of Christ?" or "How many souls have we reached with the Gospel?" or "How esteemed are we in the eyes of men?" or "At what leadership level are we?" or "What are our accomplishments?" The question, according to the standard of the Word of the living God, is, "Have we begun? Have we the fear of the Lord?"

How do we obtain the fear of the Lord?

1. *We make it a choice with our will.* We say, "I want this because I see my desperate need of it." Proverbs 1:29 says, "They hated knowledge and did not choose the fear of the LORD."

2. *We confess our lack of the fear of the Lord before God and cry out to God to have mercy upon us.*

3. *We continually seek God for the fear of the Lord with intense desire and receive it by faith.* In Hebrews 11:6 we read, "And without faith it is impossible to please him." We can cry out day and night for the fear of God, but unless we receive it by faith nothing will happen. Romans 14:23 says, "Whatever does not proceed from faith is sin." Because of who God is, we know He will delight to impart it to us. We will know the outworking of it by our new attitude toward sin; sin will be distasteful.

4. *We make a study of the fear of the Lord from the Word of God.* The best methods of study are usually listening, looking, reading, writing and meditating. When we mean business with God, we will obtain a big notebook or several notebooks. He is such a big God, and there is much to learn about His character and His ways. For many years I have been compiling a big notebook where I have written out many hundreds of Bible verses on the different aspects of the character of God and the ways of God. We start making a study of the fear of the Lord from His Word, asking Him to make us acutely aware of every Scripture on the subject. We underline the verses in our Bible. We place a heading

in our notebook, "The Fear of the Lord," and write out the verses on that subject. We meditate on them.

We read them slowly, quietly, carefully, under the illumination of the Holy Spirit, asking Him to give us understanding from His point of view on these Scriptures and to give us insight beyond the surface meaning. We receive by faith that He will.

I have found and written out more verses on the fear of the Lord than on any other subject I have studied since I started meaning business with God—simply because it is one of God's major truths. All truth from God is of utmost importance, but God has some things in His Word that He says a lot more about than others— they are His majors. A question to ask is: What are we majoring on—some minor truth or His major truths? We should be making a priority in our lives what God has made priority in His Word. What He says so much more about, we should make so much more of in our lives.

If we were an employer, for example, the employee we would promote, give more responsibility to and take into closer friendship would be the one who made a study of what was important to us, applied it and made it most important to himself. God operates in exactly the same way.

Do we want to have intimate friendship with the living God? Then we must make what is extremely important to Him extremely important to us. As we have seen, holiness is of the utmost importance to

God. "The friendship of the Lord is for those who fear him [who hate sin], and he makes known to them his covenant [or secrets]" (Psalm 25:14). This means the secrets of His Word—also the secret things that are on His heart in vision and purpose of how to reach this lost world.

The following verses tell us *how* we are to make a study of this subject from the Word of God.

> My son, if you receive my words and treasure up my commandments with you, making your ear attentive to wisdom and inclining your heart to understanding; yes, if you cry out for insight and raise your voice for understanding, if you seek it like silver and search for it as for hidden treasures; *then* you will understand the fear of the Lord and find the knowledge of God.
>
> Proverbs 2:1–5, italics added

Few people casually look for lost money! And how many would be indifferent to finding something of great value if it depended only upon their pursuit of it with diligence?

5. *Finally, we go frequently into God's special school that is related to the fear of the Lord.*

> Come, O sons, listen to me, I will teach you the fear of the Lord. What man is there who desires life, and covets many days, that he may enjoy good? Keep your tongue from evil, and your lips from speaking deceit. Depart from evil, and do good; seek peace, and pursue it.
>
> Psalm 34:11–14

We find when we take our seat in this school and begin to listen, the first thing He talks about is the tongue. We do not have to be around people too long before we know whether or not they fear the Lord. The fear of the Lord is often revealed not so much by what they say as by what they do not say. What does God say? "Keep your tongue from evil, and your lips from speaking deceit" (verse 13). Let us take that literally; God means us to. "Keep your tongue from evil"—no criticism, no judging, no unbelief, no murmuring and no pride. These are some of the marks of the fear of God. "Lips free from deceit" means 100 percent honesty 100 percent of the time.

Do we really have the fear of God? How do we measure up in the light of God's standards from His Word in relation to exaggeration? We just add one or two words and imply more than the facts. We just eliminate several words and convey something other than what was conveyed the first time we heard it. We do not give the whole story! Understatement can be as untruthful as overstatement. We repeat something someone said out of context—without giving the understanding that it was said in humor or without giving other things they said before or afterward. Therefore we do not convey the right impression or 100 percent truth. *Some facts alone do not necessarily convey the truth.*

One day as I was teaching on the subject of intercession on a TV program in the United States, I was convicted by the Holy Spirit of the sin of exaggeration. I had been using an illustration out of my life to explain a point, and I had added three or four words to my true story to make it sound humorous.

159

I knew God was requiring of me to acknowledge my sin right there, repent of it and ask for His forgiveness. I did so knowing that there would be no authority on my subsequent teaching if I did not deal with it immediately.

To say *anything* that we do not mean is less than 100 percent honest.

A typical example of this is when we are asked to go somewhere with someone and we *do not want* to go. We may even have legitimate reasons for not going. Instead of just graciously declining the invitation, we insert the words, "I would *love* to go, but . . ." We have then lied and manifest our lack of the fear of the Lord.

So many times we are more concerned in speaking what we think the other person wants to hear than in what we know is truth.

It is not enough just to speak the truth for us to have the fear of God, for "grace and truth came through Jesus Christ" (John 1:17). We also see that a loving heart must always accompany truth, "speaking the truth in love" (Ephesians 4:15). As we closely study the life of the Lord Jesus, we find that He expressed grace and love with truth in a variety of ways. These were never sentimental, syrupy communications.

Paul said, "Let your speech always be gracious, seasoned with salt, so that you may know how you ought to answer every one" (Colossians 4:6).

Another way to learn the fear of the Lord in God's school of Psalm 34 is found in verse 14: "Seek peace, and pursue it." This tells us how to be a communicator who brings unity. We should never be a communicator of disunity. We should not go to Bill and tell him that Fred does not like him, does not approve of him, does not trust him or does not have confidence in him. We should not go to one brother and say another brother has given a negative comment about him.

We should be a carrier of the positive. When we hear a brother make a loving comment about another person, we could ask God to give us an opportunity to go to that person and say, "I heard the loveliest thing about you the other day. My, that brother appreciates and loves you." As we pass on comments that will help to bring peace between members of the Body of Christ, we are then "seeking peace and pursuing it." This is running after peace. It is longing and looking for, being available and yearning for opportunities to be a peacemaker among the brethren. When we are like that, we have the fear of the Lord upon us. If we know nothing of this, the fear of God is not operating in our lives as God intended it. "And the way of peace they do not know. There is no fear of God before their eyes" (Romans 3:17–18).

The greatest challenge I know of—and a sure way to have the fear of the Lord—is to dare to choose to live by the standard of the Bible. We recognize this standard as the highest. We may see very little of it as the lived-out standard of others—even among spiritual leaders. But we have the opportunity of choosing the standard of our model, the Lord Jesus Christ, who delighted in the fear of the Lord (see Isaiah 11:3).

We may well be called a fanatic or an extremist if we do. Second Timothy 3, verse 12 says, "Indeed all who desire to live a godly life in Christ Jesus will be persecuted." This is a promise from God, so expect it. Sadly enough, often the greatest persecution comes from other Christians who do not choose the same standard.

What will be the reward for our choice? Intimate friendship with God! More than enough reward!

But we may say, "How can we speak the truth 100 percent of the time and yet be gracious and loving?"

Answers are found in the next chapter.

17

The Source of Wisdom

"But where shall wisdom be found? And where is the place of understanding? . . . And he said to man, 'Behold, the fear of the Lord, that is wisdom; and to depart from evil is understanding'" (Job 28:12, 28). Wisdom is part of the package when we have the fear of God. Now that is good news!

Many years ago when I started studying this subject, it was a tremendous discovery for me to find how I could obtain wisdom. All my life I had been impressed with my lack of natural wisdom. I desperately wanted wisdom, but did not know how to get it. Although I had been surrounded by good Bible teaching all my life, I cannot recall hearing a message on the fear of the Lord. Even if the Bible teachers did not teach it, I cannot blame them. I can only blame myself, as I had the Word of God and the indwelling Holy Spirit. I could have studied. When I began to search the Scriptures daily in order to know God, I soon discovered these truths.

I not only discovered the fear of the Lord is where wisdom is found, but I also discovered I could have as much wisdom as I chose to be holy. Hallelujah! What relief. What release to submit to the Person of the Holy Spirit to work this in me and then through me to others. The fear of the Lord is not only the beginning of wisdom (Psalm 111:10), but it is instruction in wisdom (Proverbs 15:33). There will be an increase of wisdom as there is an increase in holiness.

Perhaps wisdom is never more needed than for us to know when we are to be silent and when we are to speak. In Ecclesiastes 3:7, we find there is "a time to keep silence, and a time to speak." This means there is a need for openness as well as "closedness" in our character. Only the fear of the Lord upon us will produce the wisdom to have both in equal strength.

In our openness, we need to be transparently honest, quick to admit our sins and prompt to offer forgiveness when others have wronged us. We need to share in others' joys and sorrows. We need to be good communicators of love, encouragement, comfort and understanding.

We need to be closed in relation to repeating others' sins that they have confessed privately.

We need to be careful about sharing revelation of truth. We need to be equally careful about the timing. The Holy Spirit will prompt us in relation to both. Paul had more revelation of truth than most, but he was not permitted by God to share all of it (see 2 Corinthians 12:3–4).

After Peter, James and John had been on the Mount of Transfiguration with Jesus and had received remarkable revelation, it is significant how Jesus instructed them. "And as they were coming down the mountain, he charged them to tell no one what they had seen, until the Son of man should have risen from the dead. So they kept the matter to themselves" (Mark 9:9–10).

Others have to be prepared by God to receive the revelation of truth before it is right or wise for us to share it. "He who obeys a command will meet no harm, and the mind of a wise man will know the time and way. For every matter has its time and way" (Ecclesiastes 8:5–6).

The Word of God makes it clear that an unprepared heart does not know how to handle the truth, if we speak it without God's direction to do so. "Do not give dogs what is holy; and do not throw your pearls before swine, lest they trample them under foot and turn to attack you" (Matthew 7:6).

Many times in the Gospels, Jesus commanded people not to share their testimony after He had healed them (see Mark 7:36; Luke 5:14; and Luke 8:56). Often they disobeyed Him.

We should be very strict in having closed lips in relation to other people's shared confidences. "He who goes about as a talebearer reveals secrets, but he who is trustworthy in spirit keeps a thing hidden" (Proverbs 11:13).

God has a special word of exhortation in relation to wives of unconverted husbands. God says to win them through living a Christlike life in front of them. "Likewise you wives, be submissive to your husbands, so that some, though they do not obey the word, may be won without a word *by the behavior of their wives*" (1 Peter 3:1, italics added).

Talking to God on their husbands' behalf in intercession will be so much more effective than trying to talk them into becoming a Christian.

"There is one whose rash words are like sword thrusts, but the tongue of the wise brings healing" (Proverbs 12:18).

Here is a very practical outworking of wisdom in an everyday situation. Let's say someone comes up to us and asks, "How do you like my new hairstyle?" We may think it is awful, but how will we answer? We have been learning that the fear of the Lord means lips free from deceit, and that means 100 percent truth. We will not say, "Because I have now learned the fear of God, which means I have to be totally honest with you, I must tell you I think it is awful." No, the fear of the Lord means having lips free from deceit, *with wisdom*.

One way we may answer the question is to say, "Well, there are other hairstyles I have seen on you that I like better. For instance, the way you wore your hair last month was really lovely!" We have spoken the truth here in love. We have not conveyed anything other than the fact that we do not like it; but we said it graciously. We accentuated the positive, and we eliminated the negative. As the old song that I sang as a teenager says, "Accentuate the positive, eliminate the negative, and don't mess with Mister In-between."

It may be that we have never seen another hairstyle on that person. If we have the fear of God on us, the Holy Spirit will quickly put the wise words to use into our minds. As we trust Him, and listen and learn, He speaks through us. It is an illuminating and exciting adventure.

God has not left us in any doubt about the way He is going to shower His favor upon those who choose to live by His standard of holiness. Perhaps the biggest incentive of all to make that choice permanently comes in the final chapter.

18

Rewards for Those Who Fear the Lord

One of the most superlative promises in the whole of God's Word is found in Malachi 3:16–17:

> Then those who feared the LORD spoke with one another; the LORD heeded and heard them, and a book of remembrance was written before him of those who feared the LORD and thought on his name. "They shall be mine, says the LORD of hosts, my special possession on the day when I act, and I will spare them as a man spares his son who serves him."

Now that is really something! A special book will be written about those who fear God; they will be God's special possession, and they will receive His special protection. But the most special thing that can happen to us is that we will be in intimate friendship with the most exciting, holy, fabulous, wonderful Person in the universe—King God!

That friendship results in two things:

1. It fulfills Him because that is why He created us, and
2. It fulfills us.

Do we want to fulfill God? Or do we want God to be disappointed, and do we want to be frustrated ourselves? There is nothing in between.

Every person is either fulfilled or frustrated to the degree he or she is in intimate friendship with God. There is no other way for that intimate friendship to develop outside the fear of God. It is our choice. "Let us cleanse ourselves from every defilement of body and spirit, and make holiness perfect in the fear of God" (2 Corinthians 7:1).

Will you join me in bowing before Him in this prayer?

King God, we simply state before You that we want to be known in heaven, on earth and in hell as men and women who fear the Lord. We want You to be able to give that description of us as You did about Your servants Job and Cornelius. We pray with the psalmist, "Teach me your way, O LORD, and I will walk in your truth; give me an undivided heart, that I may fear your name" (Psalm 86:11, NIV). We do not choose to be challenged by the truths in this book. We choose to be changed. We will obey the truth. Thank You that You will then set us free—free to be in intimate friendship with You—the ultimate freedom, the ultimate fulfillment. Amen.

Promises for Those Who Fear the Lord

1. Fruitfulness

   "But the midwives feared God, and did not do as the king of Egypt commanded them, but let the male children live" (Exodus 1:17).

   "And because the midwives feared God he gave them families" (Exodus 1:21).

2. Deters us from sinning

   "And Moses said to the people, 'Do not fear; for God has come to prove you, and that the fear of him may be before your eyes, that you may not sin'" (Exodus 20:20).

3. Blessings on us and on our children

   "Oh that they had such a mind as this always, to fear me and to keep all my commandments, that it might go well with them and with their children for ever!" (Deuteronomy 5:29).

4. Prolonged days

   "The fear of the LORD is the beginning of wisdom, and the knowledge of the Holy One is insight. For by me your days will be multiplied, and years will be added to your life" (Proverbs 9:10–11).

5. Preservation of life

   "The fear of the LORD leads to life; and he who has it rests satisfied; he will not be visited by harm" (Proverbs 19:23).

6. Success

"Though a sinner does evil a hundred times and prolongs his life, yet I know that it will be well with those who fear God, because they fear before him" (Ecclesiastes 8:12).

7. Deliverance

"But you shall fear the LORD your God, and he will deliver you out of the hand of all your enemies" (2 Kings 17:39).

8. Respect earned

"Ought you not to walk in the fear of our God to prevent the taunts of the nations our enemies?" (Nehemiah 5:9).

9. Given authority

"I gave my brother Hanani and Hananiah the governor of the castle charge over Jerusalem, for he was a more faithful and God-fearing man than many" (Nehemiah 7:2).

10. Taught of the Lord

"Who is the man that fears the LORD? Him will he instruct in the way that he should choose" (Psalm 25:12).

11. Friendship with God

"The friendship of the LORD is for those who fear him" (Psalm 25:14).

12. Revelation of truth

"The friendship of the LORD is for those who fear him, and he makes known to them his covenant" (Psalm 25:14).

13. Abundant goodness

"O how abundant is thy goodness, which thou hast laid up for those who fear thee" (Psalm 31:19).

14. God's attention assured

"Behold, the eye of the LORD is on those who fear him, on those who hope in his steadfast love" (Psalm 33:18).

15. Angelic protection and deliverance

"The angel of the LORD encamps around those who fear him, and delivers them" (Psalm 34:7).

16. Provision for all needs

"O fear the LORD, you his saints, for those who fear him have no want!" (Psalm 34:9).

17. Given a heritage

"For thou, O God, hast heard my vows, thou hast given me the heritage of those who fear thy name" (Psalm 61:5).

18. God's steadfast love

"For as the heavens are high above the earth, so great is his steadfast love toward those who fear him" (Psalm 103:11).

19. God's compassion

   "As a father pities his children, so the LORD pities those who fear him" (Psalm 103:13).

20. Provision of food

   "He provides food for those who fear him" (Psalm 111:5).

21. Wisdom

   "The fear of the LORD is the beginning of wisdom; a good understanding have all those who practice it" (Psalm 111:10).

22. Blessings from God

   "Praise the LORD. Blessed is the man who fears the LORD, who greatly delights in his commandments!" (Psalm 112:1).

23. Increased blessings upon us and our children

   "He will bless those who fear the LORD, both small and great" (Psalm 115:13).

   "The LORD shall increase you more and more, you and your children" (Psalm 115:14, KJV).

24. Special blessings related to family life

   "Blessed is every one who fears the LORD, who walks in his ways! You shall eat the fruit of the labor of your hands; you shall be happy, and it shall be well with you. Your wife will be like a fruitful vine within your house; your children will be like olive shoots around your table. Lo, thus shall the man be blessed who fears the LORD. The LORD bless you from Zion! May you see the prosperity of Jerusalem all the days of your life! May you see your children's children! Peace be upon Israel!" (Psalm 128).

25. Protection

"You who fear the LORD, trust in the LORD! He is their help and their shield" (Psalm 115:11).

26. Companionship of others who fear God

"I am a companion of all who fear thee, of those who keep thy precepts" (Psalm 119:63).

27. Fulfilled desires

"He fulfils the desire of all who fear him, he also hears their cry, and saves them" (Psalm 145:19).

28. God takes pleasure in us

"The LORD takes pleasure in those who fear him, in those who hope in his steadfast love" (Psalm 147:11).

29. Healing and refreshment

"Be not wise in your own eyes; fear the LORD, and turn away from evil. It will be healing to your flesh and refreshment to your bones" (Proverbs 3:7–8).

30. Confidence in God and assurance of refuge for our children

"In the fear of the LORD one has strong confidence, and his children will have a refuge" (Proverbs 14:26).

31. Ability to avoid evil

   "By the fear of the LORD a man avoids evil" (Proverbs 16:6).

32. Satisfaction

   "The fear of the LORD leads to life; and he who has it rests satisfied" (Proverbs 19:23).

33. Riches, honor and life

   "The reward for humility and fear of the LORD is riches and honor and life" (Proverbs 22:4).

34. Honor for women

   "Charm is deceitful, and beauty is vain, but a woman who fears the LORD is to be praised" (Proverbs 31:30).

35. Advancement

   "It is good that you should take hold of this, and from that withhold not your hand; for he who fears God shall come forth from them all" (Ecclesiastes 7:18).

36. Steadfastness

   "I will make with them an everlasting covenant, that I will not turn away from doing good to them; and I will put the fear of me in their hearts, that they may not turn from me" (Jeremiah 32:40).

37. Names recorded in God's book of remembrance, God's special possession and special protection

   "Then those who feared the LORD spoke with one another; the LORD heeded and heard them, and a book of remembrance was written before him of those who feared the LORD and thought on his name" (Malachi 3:16).

38. God's mercy
"And his mercy is on those who fear him from generation to generation" (Luke 1:50).

39. Acceptable to God
"In every nation any one who fears him and does what is right is acceptable to him" (Acts 10:35).

What a Commitment of Life to the Lord Jesus Christ Means

"Choose for yourselves this day whom you will serve. . . . As for me . . . [I] will serve the LORD" (Joshua 24:15, NIV).

"From one man he made every nation of men, that they should inhabit the whole earth; and he determined the times set for them and the exact places where they should live. God did this so that men would seek him and perhaps reach out for him and find him, though he is not far from each one of us" (Acts 17:26–27, NIV).

1) *Acknowledge that you are a sinner and repent of your sin.*

"For all have sinned and fall short of the glory of God" (Romans 3:23, NIV).

"Repent, then, and turn to God, so that your sins may be wiped out" (Acts 3:19, NIV).

"If we confess our sins, he is faithful and just and will forgive us our sins and purify us from all unrighteousness" (1 John 1:9, NIV).

2) *Believe Christ died and rose again to save you from your sin and to give you eternal life.*

"Christ died for sins once for all, the righteous for the unrighteous, to bring you to God" (1 Peter 3:18, NIV).

"For there is one God and one mediator between God and men, the man Christ Jesus" (1 Timothy 2:5, NIV).

"For God so loved the world that he gave his one and only Son, that whoever believes in him shall not perish but have eternal life" (John 3:16, NIV).

"Salvation is found in no one else, for there is no other name under heaven given to men by which we must be saved" (Acts 4:12, NIV).

3) *Receive Christ by faith and accept the gift God has provided in His Son.*

"Jesus answered, 'I am the way and the truth and the life. No one comes to the Father except through me'" (John 14:6, NIV).

"To all who received him, to those who believed in his name, he gave the right to become children of God" (John 1:12, NIV).

"Here I am! I stand at the door and knock. If anyone hears my voice and opens the door, I will come in" (Revelation 3:20, NIV).

"God has given us eternal life, and this life is in his Son. He who has the Son has life; he who does not have the Son of God does not have life" (1 John 5:11–12, NIV).

4) *Commit your whole life to the Lord Jesus Christ and follow Him and serve Him without reserve.*

"Whoever believes in the Son has eternal life, but whoever rejects the Son will not see life, for God's wrath remains on him" (John 3:36, NIV).

"If anyone would come after me, he must deny himself and take up his cross and follow me" (Matthew 16:24, NIV).

"Anyone who loves his father or mother more than me is not worthy of me; anyone who loves his son or daughter more than me is not worthy of me; and anyone who does not take his cross and follow me is not worthy of me" (Matthew 10:37–38, NIV).

"'I tell you the truth,' Jesus said to them, 'no one who has left home or wife or brothers or parents or children for the sake of the kingdom of God will fail to receive many times as much in this age and, in the age to come, eternal life'" (Luke 18:29–30, NIV).

5) *Be prepared to confess Christ and to tell others that you belong to Him.*

"If you confess with your mouth, 'Jesus is Lord,' and believe in your heart that God raised him from the dead, you will be saved. For it is with your heart that you believe and are justified, and it is with your mouth that you confess and are saved" (Romans 10:9–10, NIV).

"Whoever acknowledges me before men, I will also acknowledge him before my Father in heaven. But whoever disowns me before men, I will disown him before my Father in heaven" (Matthew 10:32–33, NIV).

"If anyone is ashamed of me and my words, the Son of Man will be ashamed of him when he comes in his glory and in the glory of the Father and of the holy angels" (Luke 9:26, NIV).

6) *Acknowledge that the Lord Jesus not only died upon the cross to give you eternal life, but that He rose again from the dead to live His life in you and through you.*

"Christ in you, the hope of glory" (Colossians 1:27, NIV).

"I have been crucified with Christ and I no longer live, but Christ lives in me. The life I live in the body, I live by faith in the Son of God, who loved me and gave himself for me" (Galatians 2:20, NIV).

My Prayer of Committal of Life to the Lord Jesus Christ

"Lord Jesus, I know that I am a sinner. I turn away from my sin, in repentance, and ask You to forgive me. I believe You died on the cross for my sin and I thank You with all my heart. I now invite You to come into my heart and life. By faith, I receive You as my Savior, and make You my Lord and Master. I place my whole life in Your hands without reserve. Thank You that You not only died to give me the gift of eternal life, but that You rose again to live Your life in me and through me. I am prepared to acknowledge You as my Lord before others, and in constant dependence upon the Holy Spirit live for You, in obedience to Your promptings. Thank You that according to Your Word You have come in and made me Your child. Thank You that You have cleansed and forgiven me for my sin, and given me eternal life." Amen.

Essentials for Progress as a Christian

1) *Daily prayer as well as daily reading of God's Word is absolutely essential for you to grow spiritually strong.*

You could start by reading the Gospel of John and the Psalms. Ask God the Holy Spirit to give you understanding and then thank Him that He will.

"Without faith it is impossible to please God, because anyone who comes to him must believe that he exists and that he rewards those who earnestly seek him" (Hebrews 11:6, NIV).

Underline a verse when God speaks to you from it. The Bible is your guide and map.

"Your word is a lamp to my feet and a light for my path" (Psalm 119:105, NIV).

Do not confine prayers to "asking" but include thanksgiving and praise.

"With thanksgiving, present your requests to God" (Philippians 4:6, NIV).

"Praise him for his acts of power; praise him for his sur-passing greatness" (Psalm 150:2, NIV).

2) *Seek God's guidance in all things and expect Him to give it.*

"I will instruct you and teach you in the way you should go; I will counsel you and watch over you" (Psalm 32:8, NIV).

He has promised to speak to us.

"My sheep listen to my voice; I know them, and they fol-low me" (John 10:27, NIV).

3) *Meet regularly with other keen Christians in the church fellowship to which God leads you.*

"They devoted themselves to the apostles' teaching and to the fellowship, to the breaking of bread and to prayer" (Acts 2:42, NIV).

"Let us not give up meeting together, as some are in the habit of doing, but let us encourage one another" (Hebrews 10:25, NIV).

4) *An important method of public witness is to experience believer's baptism.*

"As they traveled along the road, they came to some water and the eunuch said, 'Look, here is water. Why shouldn't I be baptized?'" (Acts 8:36, NIV).

By this we make an open confession of our faith in the Lord Jesus Christ in the way in which He commanded us.

"Go and make disciples of all nations, baptizing them in the name of the Father and of the Son and of the Holy Spirit" (Matthew 28:19, NIV).

5) *Seek opportunities to lead others to Christ.*

"He who wins souls is wise" (Proverbs 11:30, NIV).

"'Come, follow me,' Jesus said, 'and I will make you fishers of men'" (Matthew 4:19, NIV).

6) *Remember that your enemy, the devil, and his demons will attack you in many ways, trying to make you sin.*

"Submit yourselves, then, to God. Resist the devil, and he will flee from you" (James 4:7, NIV).

"The one [the Lord Jesus Christ] who is in you is greater than the one [the devil] who is in the world" (1 John 4:4, NIV).

7) *Should you fall into sin, do not be discouraged, but in repentance confess all to the Lord.*

"Everyone who confesses the name of the Lord must turn away from wickedness" (2 Timothy 2:19, NIV).

8) *Be filled with the Spirit* (see Ephesians 5:18).

God the Holy Spirit is a Person who wants to completely control your life, so that the Lord Jesus Christ may be made real to you, and then through you to others.

Without His control you will be a powerless, ineffective Christian.

> a) *Surrender your will totally to God.*
> "The Holy Spirit, whom God has given to those who obey him" (Acts 5:32, NIV).

> b) *Be thorough in confession and repentance of all known sin.*

185

"He who conceals his sins does not prosper, but whoever confesses and renounces them finds mercy" (Proverbs 28:13, NIV).

c) *Ask God to fill you with His Spirit.*
"If you then, though you are evil, know how to give good gifts to your children, how much more will your Father in heaven give the Holy Spirit to those who ask him!" (Luke 11:13, NIV).

d) *Believe that He will, and thank Him for doing so.*
"Everything that does not come from faith is sin" (Romans 14:23, NIV).

Allow the Holy Spirit to manifest Himself in whichever way He chooses, by being obedient to His promptings.

These conditions need to be fulfilled constantly in order to maintain the Spirit-filled life.

Joy Dawson has been traveling internationally and teaching the Bible since 1970, mostly at spiritual leadership conferences. Her missionary journeys have taken her to 55 nations and every continent.

She has taught extensively on television and radio, and countless lives have been eternally touched through the worldwide distribution of her books and audio- and videotapes. The character and ways of God are the biblical basis of her penetrating teachings, which cross denominational lines.

Joy and her husband, Jim, with their two married children and four adult grandchildren and their partners, are full-time missionary leaders with Youth With A Mission, an interdenominational missionary organization operating in 173 nations. Their son, John, is the president of YWAM.

Jim and Joy are elders of The Church On The Way in Van Nuys, California, and are members of America's National Prayer Committee.

Hear Joy Dawson teach on almost 200 different key subjects.

Ideal for training schools, Bible institutes, churches, home groups or private study.

For your free Resource Guide, contact:

Los Angeles Youth With A Mission
11141 Osborne Street
Lake View Terrace, CA 91342

Phone: (818) 896-2755
Fax: (818) 897-6738
Email: info@ywamla.org
Website: www.ywamla.org

Evangelism—
Simple and Natural

Evangelism is not an assignment, a punishment, or a duty. It is an overflow of God's life in you that brings more life in turn—first to you and then to those with whom you share. This book will be a tool to enlighten you and empower you for one of the greatest privileges and some of the most rewarding interchanges you will ever have in this life.

Spirit-Led Evangelism will transform your thinking, ignite your heart for the lost, and show you just how simple and natural personal evangelism can be.

"I can't think of anyone who wouldn't greatly benefit from reading this outstanding book. It's that relevant and potent! I am reading it for the second time."
—Joy Dawson, YWAM

Spirit-Led Evangelism by Ché Ahn
Available May 2008

Remove Barriers to Victorious Living

Millions of Christians across the globe are constantly battling the sin in their lives—and losing. But in his book *Roll Away Your Stone*, Dutch Sheets offers hope through powerful and life-changing biblical truths about who you are in Christ and how to become the person God made you to be—a conqueror.

More than a book about identity in Christ, this is an action plan to conquer the lies that keep Christians defeated and to see themselves as they are in God's eyes. In *Roll Away Your Stone*, you'll find sound, easy-to-use tools for understanding God, His provisions, and the principles He has established that enable you to be set free and walk in His way.

Roll Away Your Stone by Dutch Sheets